To Aunty Maude
with love

Living in Hope

Margaret Plummer Russell

authorHOUSE®

AuthorHouse™ UK Ltd.
500 Avebury Boulevard
Central Milton Keynes, MK9 2BE
www.authorhouse.co.uk
Phone: 08001974150

© 2008 Margaret Plummer Russell. All rights reserved.

No part of this book may be reproduced, stored in a retrieval system, or transmitted by any means without the written permission of the author.

First published by AuthorHouse 9/15/2008

ISBN: 978-1-4343-9560-3 (sc)

Printed in the United States of America
Bloomington, Indiana

This book is printed on acid-free paper.

Contents

Part 1 Family Story..1
  Chapter 1 Ramsbottom.......................................3
  Chapter 2 Buckhurst..20

Part 2 Margaret's Story 31
  Chapter 1 Jericho Workhouse—bury 33
  Chapter 2 Kirkham Children's Home................38
  Chapter 3 Queensferry, North Wales................48
  Chapter 4 Minster Lodge, Ormskirk, Lancs. 53
  Chapter 5 Bootle, Liverpool 57
  Chapter 6 The Hunt For My Family 79
  Chapter 7 Dad 86
  Chapter 8 Revisits To My Previous Homes..........90

Part 3 Hugh's Story 105
  Chapter 1 107

Part 4 Alice's story 127
  Chapter 1 Ramsbottom....................................129
  Chapter 2 Jericho 136
  Chapter 3 Queensferry......................................139
  Chapter 4 Liverpool 141
  Chapter 5 Nottingham......................................147
  Chapter 6 Accrington..157
  Chapter 7 Nottingham-again 159

Part 5 James' Story 175
  Chapter 1 177
  Chapter 2 Reunion..190
  Chapter 3 Revisits 199

Part 6 John's Story ... 205
Chapter 1 Accrington ... 207

Part 7 Stephen's Story ... 217
Chapter 1 ... 219
Chapter 2 18 Months To 5 Years Of Age ... 225
Chapter 3 Training ... 233
Chapter 4 Working Life ... 240
Chapter 5 Courting And Marriage ... 246
Chapter 6 Cricket Field Cat Sanctuary ... 252
Chapter 7 The Search For My Family ... 256
Chapter 8 The Final Chapter ... 259
Chapter 9 Personal Reflections ... 261

Part 8 Why? ... 263
Chapter 1 Margaret's Search For The Reason Why ... 265

Part 9 ... 271
Chapter 1 The Reunion ... 273

ACKNOWLEDGMENTS ... 279

Part 1
Family Story

Written By Margaret

Chapter 1
Ramsbottom

Union Street where Margaret was born 10th November 1937

What a beautiful summers day, I have decided to sit here in the garden, and enjoy the sunshine, the grandchildren are here and I am watching them run around without a care in the world, so happy and carefree and think how so very lucky I am to be able to sit here and listen to their giggles of delight as they dash here and there, I think back to the days when their Mums were small and wondering where had all the years gone. I wonder if my mum had had the same pleasure watching her children as we had played in my grandfathers garden, my life had been so different not having the things that the children have today I feel so blessed to have been given the chance to enjoy my life, watching and sharing in the lives of the children as they grow into their own individual personalities. I start to think of what my life had been like as a child and start to dream of the rolling hills and the valleys and the little town where I was born a small town called Ramsbottom which is a lovely little town in Lancashire valley, engulfed by hills and moor land and was until the turn of the century known as the Valley of the Garlic.

A town that was a hive of industry, with about twenty cotton and paper mills scattered all around, and smoke pouring out of the chimneys. We had smoke from the steam trains, as they shunted to and fro from the goods yards in Stubbins lane

Ramsbottom used to be a very busy railway station, and years ago you could travel every day on a train direct to London. There was a toll house at the level crossing, where people had to pay to cross the line. The toll house was demolished in 1944.

Every one was so friendly here, we had one main street, called Bridge Street, and standing in the centre of the town was St.Paul's Church. If we walked towards the bottom of Bridge Street, there is the railway station. Just a little further on we cross the bridge where the river Irwell flows, and continues along the full length of the valley. At the top of Bridge St are cross roads, which lead to Bury and Bolton.

On the 10th November 1937, I was born in this little town at 6 Union Street. My parents were Margaret and Hugh Russell, they already had a son called Hugh, who was a year older than me.

Living in Hope

The house that we lived in was only small, with a living room, kitchen and scullery, upstairs we had two bedrooms, but no bathroom. On bath night, Mum would get a tin bath that hung on a nail on the wall out side by the shed, and put it on the floor, and fill it with water, in front of a big coal fire. The children would have their baths first, and we would be put to bed while our parents had theirs.

The walls of the house were made of stone, and the floors were shiny stone flags, and because of the constant scrubbing had become very shiny over the years. They could be quite slippery when wet. We had no carpets, only mats by the hearth.

Down stairs the lighting was by gas lamp with a white mantel. The amount of light was altered by pulling a chain on either side of the mantel. Up stairs we managed with a candle. Some of the houses were over crowded, and bug infested. People could not decorate as the bugs lived in the cracks in the stone. If people did try and decorate they forced the bugs into the house next door so it was agreed that no one would decorate so people Wallpamured the walls instead. These days there are many paints to over come this.

The houses them selves were only small, and were called the railway cottages.

Most of the cottages were built for the railway workers, but also for the mill workers.

Some of the houses had to share a toilet between ten houses, these were called communal toilets, and all the mums had to take turns in keeping them clean. We were lucky; our house had its own toilet at the back by the shed.

In the middle of Union Street, there was Brooke's dairy, which sold ice-cream. In summer a man would ride around Nuttall Park on a three wheeler cycle, with an ice box on the front selling their ice cream. Any ice-cream which was not sold at the end of the day, would be given free to the children who were playing in the park.

On a Friday, a man with his horse and cart, loaded with pots and pans, donkey stones for the front steps, and all sorts of household things to sell, went around the town. He was known as Pots Dewhurst.

Every working day, a Mrs. Knowles who lived in Union Street would make some potato pies in large metal trays which she would cut into pieces and sell to the workers in and around Rose Mill which was on Irwell Street. She was well-known for her black dress, black "pinny" and her money bag hidden under her pinny.

Also in Union Street was a man who could not straighten his legs and spent his time sitting on his home made trolly, pulling himself along with his hands.

To make sure the men and women were not late for work, a man carrying a long pole (known as the knocker upper), would knock on the bedroom windows, and shout its seven o-clock. The person who was being knocked up would look out of the window and shout out that they had heard him. The knocker upper whose name was Mr Robinson would then carry on along the houses

Living in Hope

until he reached the next lamp which was put out this was done every day.

If we looked down the street, we could see the trains pulling in, bringing the people from Bury and the surrounding area to work in the mills.

Shortly after this, the men would be dashing off, to work, wearing flat caps and scarves, and carrying their Billy cans and food boxes, amid the sound of clogs on the cobbles, as they hurried to their work place.

Come eight o'clock the hooters would blow letting every one know it was time to start work.

There were a lot of "do,s" and "do not,s" in the mills for the safety of the workers. The women had to wear scarves to keep their hair away from the loom and the flying shuttles. I believe a couple of women lost their hair as a result of not abiding by the rules

Many people suffered injuries, and depending on how bad they were hurt, they had to carry on working as there was no such thing as sick pay in those days. If the loom stopped for any reason, their pay stopped immediately. They were only paid while the loom was running.

The loom workers also suffered throat problems through "kissing the bobbin:" all new girls when starting work in the mills had to learn how to" kiss the bobbin"; many girls swallowed the cotton and had to cough hard to bring it back up again. they had to put their mouths over a tiny hole and suck until the cotton came through.

On one shift my Auntie Alice was hit on the head by a flying shuttle, which had steel at the end and was lucky not to have been killed.

Auntie Alice worked hard, to look after her two children Fred and Jean, as her husband my uncle Frederick had been killed at work. I believe he was crushed by a lorry. there was no compensation in those days you had to work or starve.

The workers had to learn to lip read. The noise from the looms was so loud you could not hear if people were speaking to you.

While Mum went to work we stayed with our Grandma and Grandpa they had a lovely semi detached house with rooms either side of the front door and three bedrooms upstairs. It had a big garden for us to play in. I enjoyed being at my Grand parents, my Grandpa would sit in his big arm chair by the side board. He was a well built man and always smart in a dark suit and white shirt. His hair and beard were white. Grandma was of a small build, and always wore a dark dress with a pinafore over the top, and her hair in a bun on top of her head.

If we looked over the valley, we could see the hills beyond, with Peel Tower at the top, which was built by public subscription. The tower is a monument built in memory of Sir Robert Peel the founder of the Police force who also became Prime Minister. Sir Robert Peel also repealed the Corn Laws which had caused a lot of hardship for the cotton mills. Further along is Pilgrims cross, where years ago Travellers would sit , rest and pray

Living in Hope

as they journeyed from Ramsbottom to Whalley Abbey. Where ever we look, we are surrounded by beautiful views. Little did we realize that we would be spending a lot of time here over the next few years.

1939 and war was declared, and every few days, men could be seen on the railway station, after being called up into the army, navy, or air force.

Time went by, and the Lancashire towns suffered a lot of bombing from the Germans. This was due to the factories, which were making parts for the machines, in the mills, being converted into munitions factories, which made parts for the war effort. Little Ramsbottom was hit by two Doodle Bugs in Stubbins lane, one of them hitting a bungalow just outside Ramsbottom. Most people sheltered under the stairs of their houses, or under the dining room table, as was advised by the local Government. Every one had to put tape over their windows to stop the glass flying when the bombs were dropped. Air Raid shelters were built. Air Raid wardens would tell the people to run to the shelters as there wasn't much time when the sirens sounded. These were situated at Paradise St- Factory St- and one outside the Council Offices but they were so far apart that only people who lived near, actually used them.

There was total black out with no lights at all. Air raid wardens would walk around telling people to put their lights out during the air raids. This made it very difficult to go out in the dark, due to people tripping up on the cobbled streets

I can remember being scared, one night, as the planes flew over head. I ran down to where my Mum was working nights. One of the men saw me, and asked me what I was doing on my own. I said that I wanted my Mum. He lifted me up, and sat me on a bail of cotton then went to get Mum. She took me back home to Grandma.

As the war went on a sadness spread over our valley, as people heard that men they knew had been killed or were missing. Every one dreaded getting the official letter. But everyone rallied around, as much as they could, to help each other through these terrible times.

The wives, who had lost their husbands, were now the only bread winners in the family. As a result, they had to go out to work, and despite their grieving, had to work twelve to fourteen hours, a day in order to keep their home together, and feed the children.

It was quite common, for the mother, to send the children into the country to be boarded out, and where hopefully they would be safe.

The men and women, who did not go to war, worked longer hours in the mills, and on the land, as land army girls. At times the single girls were sent to different parts of the country, growing farm produce. Food was short, as a lot of the ships were bombed, as they brought food from abroad.

Allotments sprung up every where, and gardens had their lawns taken away, and both were used by individual families, as vegetable patches, or chicken runs supplying

Living in Hope

eggs and chicken meat to their friends, when their Ration book allowance had run out.

Auntie Alice lived in number 5 Mount Street, a block of terraced houses, with a large green lawn at the front, which was shared by all the families. Normally on bonfire night, we would have had a bonfire party, on the green, and all the children would have played, while the parents stood and talked. All this had been stopped because of the war and the "total black out".

At the back of the houses were the woodlands, where all the children would play, for hours on end, and came to no harm. The boys would play soldiers with pieces of wood for guns and the girls played on rope swings.

As we walked down to Kenyon street there was Bentleys Off Licence and a bread shop together with Coulhursts butchers co-op just around the corner a sweet shop on the other side was a cobblers.and a public house, and a long side were houses with two storey at the front and three including the cellar at the back. These were known as the Cellar Dwellings ,where people who had no- where to live went I seem to remember girl went missing her name was Sheila fox I cant remember if she was ever found.. Just a little further along were two rows of houses. I think one was called Wallis street, where years ago a family called Monks had a Tripe shop, and there was also a fish and chip shop on the same block.

1939 the houses in Union Street started to be pulled down, we moved in with our Grandparents.

Margaret Plummer Russell

On the 29th Jan 1941 Hugh, my eldest brother started school at St Paul's Infant School in Crow Lane; Dad was home so took Hugh on his first day to school but Hugh did not like being left, Mum said he would soon settle down,

On the 10th November 1941, it was my turn to start school. Dad took Hugh and I together. Hugh went along to his class room and I was taken to mine. The class rooms were all divided into separate rooms by a wood and glass petition, which was on hinges and could be pushed back to make one long room. this was used for dances which I believe Mum went to with her friend Gladys Ward , before I was born ,I think the soldiers also went there when they were on leave to the dances. The main entrance to the school was from the front of the building, which was straight on to the pavement. We did not have railings in those days. As we walked in through the main door, we had a corridor which went through to the play ground.I remember my first day in school. We were given coloured crayons, and asked to draw a picture, to take home to our mums. My picture was a rainbow of beautiful bright colours All the pictures were put on the classroom wall, until it was time for us to go home. When I got home, I was so proud to show mum and dad my rainbow picture.

As we settled into school, we were asked to bring a small cloth, and a piece of soap, to wash our hands before lunch, every day. We started school every morning, with hymns and prayers, followed by breathing exercises, to expand our lungs, as a lot of children suffered chest infections due to the damp atmosphere and the dust and smoke from the mills. During P.E. class, we were asked to place a book on our heads, and walk the length of the hall, without dropping it. This was to give the children good postures. We also had handkerchief drill as a lot of children had never used a handkerchief.

I remember as Hugh and I walked to school one day when some one had given me a Mickey Mouse rubber toy and as I walked to school I dropped it between the railway lines and could not find it, I looked every time I crossed the track but no luck. As we arrived at school, we went to our own class rooms. It would not be long before playtime, and I would meet Hugh in the play ground.

I always knew when it was play time, because the teacher, Mrs West, would get a small battered pan out of a cupboard, put it on a gas ring, and make a cup of cocoa. She would then sit at her desk, with her cup and saucer, her little finger pointing out wards.

There was also a teacher called Mrs Cook who had a bad stammer and the children used to imitate her. During the morning, we were learning the alphabet, and the teacher called me to the front of the class, and asked me to show her how I wrote a letter B, capital first, with small next. No matter which way I wrote it, she said it was wrong. All the children started to laugh at me, and I started to cry. At playtime they started calling me names. I wanted my Mum, to tell her what had happened. We talked about this at home, when we were having our tea, at the big table. Mum said every thing would be alright the next day. After tea I went to play out side, it had started to rain, so I got Grandpas umbrella and sat underneath it, just listening to the rain as it fell. Mum called me in but I said I was all right

After that, I did not like school very much. I was always scared of being called to the front of the class. Every day I felt so sick before school.

1942 16th July, this was the year that my sister Alice was born Mum was to find out that Alice suffered from bad chest infections, and needed a lot of looking after. Chest infections were quite common due to the damp atmosphere and the smog which came from the mill chimneys.

19t h October`1943, my brother James was born. Two extra children for Grandma to look after. I would rush home from school, and push James around the garden in his pram, with Alice sitting at the bottom. Grandma, with her ever watchful eye, making sure we did not come to any harm. How I loved being there.

On the Friday of Whit Weekend which was a bank holiday would be the whit walks, when all the children would walk around the town. Each church would start with a church service then walk around its own parish boundaries. St Paul's went along Union St, King St, Princes St, and back down Bridge St, and into the church grounds. All the girls wore white dresses with white flowers in their hair, and carried white flowers. Whether

Mum could not afford to buy me a dress I do not know but I can't remember this at all.

The night before Good Friday, we would hard boil some eggs, then paint them really bright colours, Then on Good Friday all the families would walk up to Peel Tower. The children would then roll the eggs down, in a race to get to the bottom, None of the eggs ever reached the bottom. My brother James always said that our Hugh had changed his egg, for a fresh one, because it always smashed on the way down. (I think my egg is still rolling)

On a Friday cousin Jean, Grandpa and I would walk down Kenyon St to meet Mum and Auntie Alice. We bought ice-cream from the corner shop then walked down to the bottom of the street, and sat on the little green hill by the mills and ate our ice-cream. Then it would be time for our Mums to go back to work. Some times on Saturdays I went and stayed with Auntie Alice, Jean, and Fred. We would all go to play in the woodland, at the back of the houses. I remember in the summer the girls would make daisy chains and put them around their necks.

Sunday, I would walk down Bridge St, on my way home. I would stop out side St Paul church, and watch as the children went in with their parents. How nice they all looked. Mums and dads with their hats on, the children holding on their mums and dads hands. How I wished it was me going in, with my family. Maybe one day.

9th June 1944 this was the year we had to say good – bye to our Grandpa. He died suddenly of a heart attack

Poor Grandma looked so lost on the day of the funeral. All the family and friends came to pay their last respects, and all filed past the coffin. Even the children. It was so sad. Then Grandpa was taken to rest in Park Chapel, the little church at the top of Peel Brow, Hugh and I had to go to school. He was now 9 years of age, and started running away, he hated school. After a few days, Mum was sent for, and told she will be in trouble from the school board, if Hugh did not attend. Mum took us the next day. Hugh was away as soon as mum went. Where to only Hugh knows.. I think his hiding place was Holcombe church grave yard. The headmaster sent for mum again. Poor Hugh got the cane. I could hear it as it landed on his hands. It must really hurt, but Hugh just blows on his hands. Hugh was such a thin boy, and the cane must have really hurt him he just walked back into class.

1945 This was the year John was born. It was also announced that war was over there would be celebrations and street parties. Most families would be reunited, as the men came home.. For some, it would be heart breaking, as their husbands, or fathers, had been killed or were missing,

We were in for a surprise; we were getting a visit from King George the 6th and Queen Elizabeth his consort who was to become the Queen mother. All the school walked to the top of Bridge St and waited. We were all

Living in Hope

given a small flag to wave as they went past. It was a marvellous site, all the town turned out for the occasion.

We had never seen any thing like it before. The entire town cheered as they went past. The King and Queen did a walk about and spoke to a number of people including a small boy who was born on coronation day. The King also presented a badge to a Mrs Alice Foster for all her good work with the W.R.V.S. It was soon over We then we had to go back into school and write about it. The Royal family were giving their support and encouragement to recover after the war. Mrs Doris Hillary also did her share in preparing meals for the people whose houses had been damaged

12th, Nov Grandma was taken into hospital, Mum said she would be in for a few days but after the fifth day Grandma asked to come home and on the 17th Nov was discharged into mums care. I remember it had been snowing and we had no coal for the fire Mum picked up a bucket and started to walk down the road I followed her down to the railway sidings where mum started digging with her bare hands to find coal that had fallen from the trains as they shunted along.

I had never felt so cold I was only wearing a thin dress no socks or coat. Mum said she had found some coal, not a lot but enough for a fire.

January 1947, Ramsbottom was to have a severe snow fall, and the trains were unable to deliver coal to the mills, and as a result the mills had to be closed for at least three weeks.

Margaret Plummer Russell

In February of the same year the snow drifts that hit Ramsbottom were 10ft deep, which caused an electricity crisis, and kept the mills closed. This meant great hard ship for the mill workers as there were no benefits available. As a result the Ramsbottom Weavers Association gave a grant of one pound per week per employee, to part cover lost wages. The shops had no heating and were lit by candles. 22nd February 1947, this was the year my beloved Grandma died. I had never seen so many people. Aunties and Uncles and all the neighbours had brought floral tributes when they came to say good by to our Grandma. She is buried with Grandpa at the Park Chapel, over looking the little town, where on the 21st of February 1900 they had married and later brought up their family.

I went with Mum, and put flowers on their grave, every Sunday. I watched Mum, as she tended her parent's grave. She must have felt so alone then.

When Mum finished, we started the walk down Peel Brow, to what used to be our Grandparents house. It felt so strange with out them. A few weeks later mum took over the tenancy of the house.

During the months ahead, Mum was finding it hard going. She had been given our Grandparents house, but I think she was struggling, as she could not work, with having to look after all the children. I don't think the mills had picked up since the war. A lot of the families were suffering, most were in a similar position as Mum, as they had no husbands to help them…

Living in Hope

1947 Dad came home, but not for long?.Dad took Alice on the day she started school, she didn't go much as she suffered from a bad chest, I heard mum say Alice had Bronchitis, so had to stay home from school I think the amount of time she did attend, she only learned her ABC, but at least she got her letter B, right not like me.

James started school, but only for a month or so we broke up for our summer holidays.

But our lives were going to be turned up side down. I heard Mum say that we would be leaving Ramsbottom soon, and going to a place on the moor. Quite a way from here

Over the next couple of days Mum told us that we would be leaving Ramsbottom. I would have to say good-bye, finally, to the Grandparents whose grave, I attended every Sunday with Mum and had spent so much of my early life with, and loved so very much, I thought the tears would never stop. I would not be able to see my Auntie Alice or my cousins Jean and Fred or get the chance to go into Church with my Mum or my family ,I don't know what has happened to Dad, but he hasn't been around for a while and wasn't going to be around, where had he gone ?this I was to find out many years later.

Now a new chapter of our life is to begin

CHAPTER 2
BUCKHURST

30th September 1948 to 17th March 1949

This is the day when we left our home to start a new life on the moor. I would not be able to visit or put flowers on our Grandparents grave - the grandparents with whom I had shared the early part of my life.

I loved them so very much.

How I missed their hugs and the attention they had given me, when Mum's time was so tied up with the little ones.

Some how things had not seemed the same since they had passed away.

I started to cry, but Mum said every thing would be alright, and that I would love our new home which we were going to.

We were heading for the Forgotten Valley, where many years ago was very active, with mills all along the valley and the River Irwel supplying the water which the mills needed to keep the machines turning. Then over the years the mills had gradually closed, one by one, due to modernisation of the processes. In the end the mills were not big enough for the demands, and with not enough

Living in Hope

people living on the moors, to work in them, the bigger mills in Ramsbottom and surrounding areas were used.

We started to walk up long winding country lanes, one lane leading into another. On either side of the lane were high bushes, all different colours, they were starting to get red berries on them. I asked Mum," how much further?" as we had been walking for what seemed hours, and we were all getting tired, mum said, "not long now". Mum was pushing John and James in the pram, and Alice was holding on to my hand. Hugh was way back. He did not want to move all this way, and leave behind his friends in Ramsbottom.

As we walked on, I thought of Auntie Alice, cousins Jean and Fred, and remembered the woodlands where we used to play. The excitement as bonfire night was only six weeks away, and all the children would be gathering wood for the fire, and making the guy. We would sit outside the shops, waiting for people to throw their coppers into an old hat. With the money we had collected, we would then ask the grown ups to buy the fireworks for us. How I was going to miss it all.

I tried to put my thoughts behind me, and carried on.

Mum looked very tired, I think the move was affecting her as well, but she did not say anything.

We came to the top of a hill and Mum pointed to a small grey building, a short way up the lane, it was a chapel. We were to find out later that I would be attending the chapel as a school, but on a Sunday it was used for church services.As we drew nearer, Mum told us that there was a pond, with ducks and geese, but we must not get too near, as they may biteWe turned down another lane, and in front stood our cottage, with a waterfall running alongside. To get over to our new home, we had a bridge to cross.

It was very quiet here, nothing around except a few farms in the distance. The weather was beautiful, and every where was so green and fresh. The air smelled so clean, not like the smell from the mills.

As we approached the cottage, a gentleman came over. to Mum. He said his name was Mr Kefford our next door neighbour, and that when we got settled in, he would send some eggs over, as he had hens and ducks. Mr Kefford only had one arm, he told mum he had lost his arm in the war.

We were to find out that there was no electricity, gas, or running water. The water had to be collected from the well behind the barn. The cottage was very small, with not much furniture. Along the wall, just inside the door, was a big sideboard, which took up nearly all the room, and then a kitchen. The kitchen had nothing in, only a pot sink. As we went up the stairs, which were very narrow, I noticed two bedrooms, with no furniture in "where were we going to sleep?" There was no bathroom. Somehow it reminded me of Union St., our first home. But there our house was furnished. I came down stairs again, and decided to go for a walk, taking Alice with me, while Mum saw to James and John.

We walked up the lane, passed the duck pond, and had a look at the chapel. I had not seen the bell on the roof, when we arrived. I thought how lovely it would sound, when rung on a Sunday, to tell people it was time for church.

Alice and I took a look at the ducks, but not too close. On the way back, we played by the waterfall, throwing pebbles in, but it did not make much of a splash, as there was no depth to it.

Alice decided to run ahead, but I sat by the waterfall, and took in the scenery that was all around, and listened to the sound of cows munching the grass in the field opposite. There was also a horse close by, I remember Mr Kefford, the man from next door, saying its name was Old Ned.

I walked on home, as it was getting late by this time. There was no sign of Hugh. He must have been enjoying himself, a boy's adventure. Our neighbour, Mr Kefford, told us that there were some old mines not far from the cottage. Maybe Hugh had found them, I hoped he was alright.

After a couple of days, Mum said it was time for Hugh and I to start school.

The first day, Mum took us, and we met the teacher. Her name was Mrs Cook She was very nice, the school was only small inside, and at the back of the chapel there was a communion rail, an alter and also a font for christenings.All of which were concealed during the week by a curtain that was pulled across until used on the

Sunday The pews that were used for church, were also used by the children for lessons during the week. There were about 40 children, of all different ages, being taught at the same time, by one teacher. There was also a cook. After mum left, we were given a book and pencil, and asked to write our names on the front of the book. We put our books down on the bench, and we started with a hymn and prayers, then our work would begin.

Suddenly my thoughts went back to St Paul's school, and the teacher calling me out, to the front of the class. I got this awful feeling inside, and could not settle, Soon it was time for break, and we were given a small bottle of milk, and then went out to play. If I walked to the gate, I could see the ducks, and geese, as they looked for food.

This was going to be the same routine every day, I thought. But no! Hugh could not stand being inside, and like St Paul's school, when we got to the door, he carried on running past, and let me go in on my own.

The teacher asked where Hugh was, and I said I did not know. Poor Mum was sent for, and was told to make sure Hugh went to school. Hugh started getting up early, so as not to see Mum, but when he came home for tea, Mum gave him a good telling off. He took no notice.

I went off to school as usual, but at lunch time, Hugh said Mum had gone into hospital, and as Dad was not a round, I would have to look after the little ones.

Some weeks later, Mum came home with a baby, wrapped up in a white blanket. Mum said the babies name was Stephen. He was born on the 9th October 1948.

As we had no cot, Mum laid him in the bottom drawer of the sideboard. and said we could hold him, when he woke up. He looked very tiny as he lay there.

October 19th James was to have his 5th birthday and on the 26th John was to have his 3rd birthday but birthdays have never meant anything to us as we have never celebrated them

The time went by so quickly, on the moor, even though there was not a lot to do, apart from walking up and down the lanes, looking for things that we might have missed before. We watched the farmers as they gathered in the hay for their cattle, over winter.

Soon it would be bonfire night; I started to think about my Auntie Alice and cousins Jean and Fred and all our friends in Ramsbottom. They would be getting ready to make their bonfire out side Auntie Alice, s house. How we were going to miss it this year; may be some of the farmer's children would have one.

Five days later it was my birthday, but I did not expect any thing.Mum asked Mr Kefford from next door, if he would mind the young children while Mum and I went to the shops.(It was to be the first time we had been off the moor since we arrived). He said he would look after Alice, James, and John, and they could help him to collect the eggs, while Mum and I and baby Stephen went down to the shop, which was quite a long walk.

Because we were on our own, it didn't seem as far as when we arrived.

Mum went inside, and bought the things that she needed. When Mum came out, she handed me a paper bag, and inside a little doll. I remember seeing it in the window. It cost 7/6. In today's money, it would be 30p, but in those days, it was an awful lot of money, that could have gone towards the shopping for food.

I felt guilty for taking it; the present should have been for John and James, Mum said it was all she could afford. I treasured that doll, it was the only present I had had in a long time.

Little did I know, it was to be the last present Mum would ever buy for me, or any of the children?

We walked back home, I kept looking at my doll, and then put it in the pram, by Stephen, as we walked over the bridge.

The children came running to meet us. Mr Kefford said they had been no trouble. I hid the doll from Alice, as I didn't want to upset her.

I still attended school, but as yet I had no warm clothes to wear. All the other children had nice warm coats. The weather was now starting to get colder.

Mum tried to keep the fire going with wood that we collected from around the cottage. We still had to get washed in cold water. I can not remember having a hot meal, as we had no cooker for Mum to use. She did her best; I think she relied on what Mr Kefford could send in from the chickens. We still had no beds to sleep in;

Living in Hope

we slept on the stone floor, on bits of bedding that Mum could get. The floor was really cold, and I slept on the out side, with my arms around the little ones, to try and keep them warm. My brother Hugh still went missing, the cold does not seem to bother him.

We had the nit nurse on her usual visit, to the school and over the next few days, the authorities called around to check that the school was safe, as the building was very old.

We were nearly into December, and Christmas would be here. The teacher said we had to learn Christmas carols to sing on Christmas Eve. But we will not celebrate as Mum has no money. Dad has not been around for a long time.

School closed for Christmas and we went back in January.

It was so quiet and cold. Mum lit candles as it got dark; it would be cosy under different circumstances; listening to the wood crackling as it burnt in the hearth.

During the day it was too cold for the little ones to play out, as they, like me had no warm clothes. Mum sometimes has to wash the clothes we wear, and try to get them dry for us to wear the next day.

Early January, and we had a severe snow fall. The school did not open, as the Lorries could not get up the lanes to deliver food, for the school children, who would normally stay for lunch. Until the snow melted, we had to stay home.

Mid-January and school re- opened. I got ready for school, but Alice wanted to come with me, but Mum said "no". I carried on over the bridge. Alice got hold of my skirt, she would not let go. I walked up the lane, with Alice holding on fast. When I walked into school, I explained to the teacher that Alice would not leave me. The teacher said she could stay, if she was quiet and gave her a book and crayons, but Alice had a nasty cough, and was disturbing the children.

Alice still suffered a lot with her bad chest. Mum thought that the fresh air up there would have been good for her, but not so far, it was far colder than we thought it would be.

We had a sewing lesson, and we were asked who knew how to do back stitch. I put my hand up, and I was asked to demonstrate to the rest of the class. I started sewing backwards. I felt so proud; I was showing the class how it was done. I was wrong. The teacher then showed the class how to sew the right way. No matter what I do turns out to be wrong. I told Mum what I had done, "Never mind" she said "everyone has to learn".

February arrived and the weather got no better. It had started to snow again but it was no where as bad as before. Up here, it is very open, (I feel so sorry for the cattle,) as they have no shelter, but I am told they are used to it.

We don't see a great deal of Hugh. He had made new friends of his own age. I cannot think what they get up to. I found it hard, as I had no girls of my age around there

I looked out of the cottage window, and thought back to the day when we had arrived. The sun had been so warm, and the grass all different shades of green. Some how thinking of the sun, made me feel warm inside. Then I remembered the waterfall running free, where as now, it was all frozen. The poor ducks and geese had to have part of the ice broken for them, so they could look for food.

Mum was looking weary, the food was very low, and mum said we were going to the market for shopping, but when we arrived the shops and market were closing. We were all so hungry to get food we scrambled under the stalls to pick up what we could find to eat, the men of the stalls were shouting for us to "clear off".

We started the long walk back home; it was nearly dark when we arrived back on the moor. We were so cold and hungry. Poor Mum was trying so hard.

What had happened to Dad, why had he left Mum to cope with all the children?

I went to school; John smiled and stood by the door, to wave to me, as he always did, until I was out of sight.

The weather had improved, but was still very windy..

March 1949 came, and we had visitors to the school, the usual nit nurse, and the firemen, to check for safety.

On the 15th of March, we had the NSPCC visit the school.

On the 17th of March two ladies, came and talked to the teacher, I was called over.

One of them said that I had been chosen to go on a holiday with them, and that I was to leave right away.

I asked could I see my Mum, but they said no, "Mum already knew" and I had to go with them.

That was the last time I was to see my family for a very long time

The last time I would see my brother John wave to me as I left to go to school.

I never knew who these people were.

What right had they to split a complete family?

We may have been poor, but we were so happy up there, and loved.

Part 2
Margaret's Story

CHAPTER 1
JERICHO WORKHOUSE—BURY

Margaret aged 3

17*th* March 1949 to April 1949

As the two ladies and I travelled down in the car, I could not help but think of Mum, and the children. The last time I saw John, he was waving to me, and smiling his lovely smile, as I walked up the lane to school. John was only three years old

We were driving along roads, which I did not know. We had always walked across fields, at Buckhurst. My thoughts were suddenly broken, as we stopped outside a long, red building. The building had a long veranda, right across the front, with a lot of smaller buildings around it.

I was taken inside, and asked to wait in a room; with one of the ladies. it must have been obvious that I was very frightened. The other lady went into another room, and when she came back, she was with another lady who had a white dress on. I think she was the matron.

I was asked my name, and asked to follow her into yet another room, where I was given something to eat.

When I had finished, I was given a night dress, and taken to a bathroom. It had cream painted walls, and the bath was in the middle of the room. I was told to take a bath, and when I had finished, I remember being shown to a very long room, with beds down both sides.

Ladies were sitting on chairs at the side of the beds, and they never said a word when I walked in. I did not like it there.

I was the only child in the room.

I climbed into bed.

I had never been away from my family before.

I felt so frightened and alone.

"What had I done that was so wrong, to have been taken away from my family?".

I wanted my Mum, "Did she know I was in Jericho Work house, and not on holiday as I had been told ?"

I cried myself to sleep, thinking that may be tomorrow Mum would come to take me home.

The next day I had breakfast, and was told not to bother the ladies.

"Why had Mum let this happen?"

I found out that Jericho Workhouse, was where people with little, or no money went, when they had no where to go, and had fallen on bad times.

Some of the people in there, had had good jobs, and through no fault of their own, had lost them, and ended up in this place.

A day or so later, I was joined by Alice, James, and Hugh; I asked them if they knew what had happened to Mum. But they said "No"

A few days after us meeting up again, the matron said we were all to go out together for the day. We were picked up and driven to a very large building. I think it was in Bury. I can still see that building in my mind; we had to walk up many steps. Inside it was very big, with a lot of doors leading off to other rooms.

We were all shown into a room, which had a large desk, and behind it sat a well built man, in a grey suit and white shirt.

I remember he had small glasses, on the end of his nose. He never spoke, just looked at us. He had a gold pen in his hand, which he placed on a big piece of blotting paper He then said he had to leave the room. I told the children not to touch any thing, I don't know why, but I thought he was testing us, to see if we took the shiny pen. He got a shock when he came back, and saw the pen had not been touched.

Hugh and I were asked to leave the room, while he spoke to Alice and James. Alice and James were very upset, when we went back in. I held their hands, and said everything would be alright. I never found out why he spoke to them alone or what had been said.

We were then all taken back to Jericho workhouse.

After we arrived back, Hugh said he did not like this place, and was going to run away, at the first chance. He was true to his word; he did. Where he went to, no one knew. I thought he may try and get back to the cottage, and Mr. Kefford,(who lived next door)

I hoped he would be alright, as it was starting to get dark.

That was the last time I saw Hugh, for a very long time.

After Hugh had gone, every day I would take Alice and James for a walk around all the small buildings, looking for Mum, just in case she had been brought there, but no one knew my Mum, and I was told to take the children back to the ward. I still took care of the children.

Alice and James would cry for Mum, day after day, but what could I do. I was only eleven years old. All I could do was to hug them, and tell them every thing would be alright, as Mum had always said to me, when ever I had been upset. Yet in my heart of hearts, I knew it would never be.

After a few days with Alice and James, I was told that I would soon be leaving.

Where to? I had not been told.

A couple of days later, I was told to get ready.

I told Alice and James. They were both crying, and holding on to me. James wanted to come, but the lady that had arrived to take me, said no. He was really crying, but she took no notice. I told James I would not be long,

All I could do was to give them one final hug, and I had to leave.

Who would look after them now? After all, to me, they were only babies of five and six years of age, when if ever would I see them again.

CHAPTER 2
KIRKHAM CHILDREN'S HOME

KIRKHAM, LANCS

April 1949 to August 1949

Once again I was on the move. I was told that I was going to Blackpool for a holiday. I had been told this once before, and had ended up in Jericho workhouse and so did not believe it. I wondered "where to this time?"

We finally arrived, and the lady I had travelled with said we had reached the place where I would be staying. As we got out of the car, I noticed the large gardens in front of the house with trees and bushes all around.

We rang the bell and a lady opened the door. She invited us in, and we walked through a porch with dark green tiles on the wall, and came to a door with beautiful coloured glass. We were offered some biscuits and a drink and I was told that she was the matron. Her name was Mrs Barfield she seemed quite nice.

I had never travelled so far before. We had always walked every where. The matron gave me a book and crayons from a cupboard in the room, and asked me to draw a picture, while she spoke to the lady who had

Living in Hope

brought me. I was then taken through a back door, to a row of houses where all the children lived.

I think I was taken to number seven.

I met all the children, but I felt so alone. All the children new each other, but I was the new girl.

I was introduced to the house mother, and she showed me round the house. The bed room, which was called a dormitory by the girls, was a big room with beds down each side. The staircase was very wide with carpets, and as we came down the stairs, we went into the dining room. There was one long table in the middle of the room, and the floor was bare varnished floor boards.

Out side there was a play area, with swings and a seesaw, and lots of space for ball games.

When the house mother had finished showing me around, she explained that all the children had jobs to do, and that we worked on a rota system. I did not know what rota meant, but I soon learned it was taking turns in doing the jobs.

She told me that all the children had to be up by seven-o-clock in the morning, and had to turn the sheets on the bed back to air. Children who had wet their beds had to take the rubber sheet off their beds, and wash them before breakfast, so that the sheets would be dry for the night time. We then got dressed and went down for breakfast, which was usually porridge or a boiled egg. After breakfast, all dishes had to be washed and the table laid for lunch. Then it was back up stairs to make their beds, when all this was done, they then got ready for school. The children who went to school had to assemble out side number seven house at 8-45 on the dot. Mr Beardsworth would blow a whistle, and if any one was late arriving they would get a smack or were caned. The children were given an apple to take for break, as the home had apple and pear trees in the grounds

12-o-clock was school lunch time, and the children had to walk back to the home. As well as having lunch, there was time for a few jobs to be done, like washing the dishes before heading back to school, which started at 1-30.At 3-30 School finished for the day and all the children walked back to the home, where they changed out of their uniform and had time to enjoy a short break.. Then it was time to get ready for tea at 5-o-clock.

After tea the clogs and shoes that had been worn that day had to be cleaned and polished ready for the next day. Like wise socks had to be washed and dried for school. The older children had to make the porridge for breakfast and depending on who made it, you could either cut it with a knife, as it was over cooked or it was like water. Either way we ate it. Again the same routine, the dishes pots and pans had to be washed before going to bed.

Come the weekend the floors had to be polished or scrubbed. In the bedrooms the floor was polished, and a piece of candlewick bedspread placed in the middle. Then there was a pot or chamber that was used in the night, so that you did not have to go along the landing to the toilet. Because we only had a small light on, some times the children would slip, and the pot would spill all over the polished floor. Then it was punishment of smacking or the slipper for the ones who had done it.

One of the girls called Norma was down for scrubbing the corridor, she thought that she would miss a bit, but it was noticed and she had her arms smacked and told to do it again. On Saturdays we wore clogs to "knock around" in. When they wore out and were sent off for repair, we were never sure that we would get the same clogs back. As long as they fitted us we wore them, if they were not too small.

By this time, I was feeling very tired as a lot had happened that day, but I still had the socks to wash before I could go to bed.

I went to bed but could not sleep. All I could think about was my family. Alice and James at Jericho and what had happened to Hugh.

Had they been moved from Jericho?

Were they still in the workhouse?

Who was looking after them?

What had happened to our Mum and Dad? Were they thinking about us?

I cried so hard that I did not think anyone could feel so hurt.

What had we done that was so wrong for this to have happened to us?

It was a very long night, I could not sleep.

Morning came, and we all made our beds and went down for breakfast After breakfast, it was my turn to wash the dishes with two other girls. One of the ladies asked me who had shown me how to wash the dishes, I said, "my Mum and Grandma" She said that I had done a good job of the plates and cutlery.

The days went by very quickly when we were not at school. All though we had some time to play, a lot of our time was doing the chores around the house.

During one of these days I was taken to the matron's office by the house mother, and sitting in the office was Alice, my sister. I could not believe it. I asked her if she knew where James was, but she could not tell me.

"The two of us are together now; at least until we are parted again," I thought to my self, "I do not mind staying here now, I have my sister to look after, and at least we are together".

The day came for me to start school. The uniform was grey with white shirts and black knee length socks with black shoes. The house mother took me the first day along with Alice and three other children from the home on the 26th April 1949.

We went to Wesham C.E of school; it was quite a long walk. We walked passed the baths, and over the railway bridge, and then followed a bend in the road, and arrived at the school. The school had one single gate from the road, and was a lot smaller than St Paul's in Ramsbottom but bigger than Buckhurst. There, we were surrounded by fields and farms. I remember thinking to my self that at Buckhurst, we only had a short country lane to walk down to my school, where as here at Kirkham I could easily get lost if I was not careful.

All these changes in my life in such a small space of time. Being parted from my family with no time to say good by was the worst thing that could happen to any child. Not knowing where my family was and not knowing if or when I would ever see them again or when I would ever get over it. Being taken from my family home to a workhouse, and then to a children's home all with in a few weeks had a devastating affect on my life.

At lunch time, we went back to the home for dinner, and then the long walk back to school. In those days, we had one and a half hours for lunch break

I thought that every day was going to be the same, until one day the house mother put me in charge of a younger child.

I would take her to school every day from now on.

I became very fond of this little friend of mine, despite me never wanting to get close to any one again.

It was a week or two later, when all the children were called into the house and asked to stand in a line. Some people came and walked up and down the line, looking at us all in turn. When they had finished we were told we could go out side again and play.

I felt that we were being put on display for people to pick who they wanted, with out us having a say whether we wanted to go or not. I soon realized that this often happened, where children disappeared and went to live with other families.

I found out later that my little friend had been chosen to go to a new mummy and daddy, and had already left with them.

Why is it when I get close to some one, they are taken away from me? Every home had its bully, and if they did not like you for some reason, then you had to watch out. I remember that once a week we had a sweet allowance. We really looked forward to getting it, but I never did. I had to hand them over to the bullies, other wise they would take it out on Alice and I would not have that happen.

Some time later a new girl called Jean arrived. She was the same age as myself I made friends with her. After a few days she convinced me that she knew where my mum was living, and that she could take me, but not to mention it to any one.

On the Saturday morning Alice, Jean and my self went out onto the main road and started to walk. I could not wait to see Mum's face when she saw us. We walked for most of the morning and Alice was getting tired. In the afternoon I slowly began to realize that Jean did not know where we were going. We had walked for most of the day, when I saw two ladies a head of us. I asked them could they help us find our mum. They said they would and invited us into their home for an ice-cream. While we were eating our ice-cream, one of the ladies went into another room and phoned the police. They had heard on the radio that three girls had run away from Kirkham

Living in Hope

Children's Home. You guessed it, the police arrived and back to the home we went.

When we arrived back we were taken straight to the matron's office, where she asked Alice and I if we were alright. I said "yes" and then she told us that Jean had done the same thing in the previous home where she had been living. We do not know what happened but we did not see Jean for some time after that.

On a Friday night, we had to line up in the kitchen for our weekly dose of liquorice." To keep our bowels regular" matron said. When matron turned her back we poured it down the sink; the smell was awful and made us all feel sick.

Sunday and we all got ready for church wearing our grey uniform. We all walked in crocodile file, some of us went to St Michael's church and we went to Wesham church. As we walked into Wesham church and looked right we looked down the aisle to a beautiful arch way in front of the choir stalls across the top was a lovely filigree design. The atmosphere was so peaceful. At the side of the church was a small gate that took us back into Wesham School.

During the week, matron said I would be going out for the day, and the lady who had taken me to the home was coming to pick me up. The lady told me we were going to Bury and there was a chance that I might see my mum.

I was so excited. "Did this mean that all my family would be getting back together again, and going back to our home on the moor, to see once again the little chapel and the ducks on the pond?"

To make conversation, I was asked to look for land marks, for the lady to look for on the way back, in case she got lost.

"Was she trying to tell me that I would not be making the journey back with her?" "Would I in fact be going home with my mum?"

We arrived at a big building, with a lot of steps up to the front door. We were somewhere in Bury, and we were shown into room, which had a big table in the middle. There were a lot of people in the room and we were asked to take a seat at the back. I looked around for mum but I could not see her. The lady, who by now I had come to look on as my friend, gave me a sweet. I remember it was a humbug which tasted lovely. I put the paper that smelled of mint in my pocket. When the talking was over, I was told that I would not be going back to mum.

"Did that mean just to day?"

"If not would I ever see my mum again?"

I never spoke all the way back to the home; in my mind were a million questions which were still unanswered.

That night I went to bed rubbing that piece of toffee paper under my nose. I could still smell the mint on it. That was the last contact with the lady I had come to know as my friend. I cried and cried that night, I thought my world had collapsed and in my heart I now new that I would probably never see my mum again. During the following week in school, I could not take my mind off the day in Bury and thought I would end up staying in the home forever, but I had one thing to be thankful for, I had Alice to look after.

It was now August and the weather was lovely and hot. We sat out side in the play ground, where we could hear the children in the swimming baths, which was next to the home. They were all enjoying them selves but we were not allowed to go.

Another day, and we are asked to stand in yet another line, as people filed past. We felt so humiliated. I stood by Alice and held her hand. We saw a lady and gentleman looking at us. We found out later that we had been chosen.

On the 8th of August, we were to leave for Queensferry in North Wales but as always I wondered for how long before we were on the move again

CHAPTER 3
QUEENSFERRY, NORTH WALES

Alice and I where taken to another home, this time in Queensferry North Wales.

This time we were going to stay with foster parents. We pulled up outside a bungalow, and a lady came out to meet us. The lady that had taken us, introduced us,

and took us into what we now know was going to be our new home, but for how long.

We were shown our bedroom. We had never had a room of our own for such a long time, It was going to feel strange sleeping on our own,.

The lady that had taken us, asked were we happy to stay for a while we said yes. Then she left.

The bungalow was in a close, just of the main road going through Queensferry.

We settled in, and then it was time for me to start school, in the September. I made some new friends, but I thought, don't get to involved, we may not be here long. But one girl in particular, seemed quite friendly, we started calling for one another to walk to school.

The weekend came, and our next door neighbour asked would we like to go to her daughters birthday party. We said yes and our Foster Mum, took us round

Living in Hope

during the afternoon. We were all asked do a party piece, but I said no, as I was always too shy , My foster Mum said I had a lovely voice, but no, I would not join in, and I was sent home, on my own and told to stay there.

When they all came home, I was told that I would not be asked again, as I was a spoil sport. But I could not help feeling the way I did. I lacked confidence, ever since I was called out in front of the class, at St Paul school. The memory of people laughing at me has always stayed with me.

Sunday, and Alice and I went to Church, morning and afternoon. Not much time for play on a Sunday- early to bed, ready for school.

On Monday morning, I met my friend and we walked to school together. During the morning, we were asked to read Corinthians in the Bible for our home work, only in Welsh.

I could not speak Welsh, and started to panic. That day all I could think of was the home work. I told my Foster parents what I had to do, but they said not to worry.I would be excused. But the day arrived and we all sat down in class, and one by one, we were asked to quote from the Corinthians. My name was called out; I just stood there, everyone looking at me. I explained to the teacher that I had never learnt Welsh in my other schools, as I was from Lancashire; I think he realized then, and told me to sit down.

Next day, as we walked to school, my friend said I had been invited back for tea, the following day, if it was all right with my Foster Parents. It was the first time I had been invited back any where, and felt so excited, and could not wait to get permission to go, I was told that I could go. So straight from school the next day, I went to my friend's house; I really enjoyed it, and felt I had been accepted. My friends Dad took me home after wards. The following day, I called for my friend but I was in for a shock. I was told she had already left for school, and not to call any more,

When I reached school, I asked my friend ,why her Mum had said not to call any more.I was told her Dads ball point pen had gone missing, and since she had not borrowed it, I must have taken it He also said that you never trust anyone from an orphanage. I felt so sick, how could anyone think like that.

I had lost my best friend for no reason. Once again, some one I got close to was taken away from me.

A couple of days later, her father came to see my Foster Mum and said that his pen had been found. He said he was sorry. But things were not the same after that.

Some time later, my foster mum gave me a present. I could use her bike, as if it were my own. I had never had such a present before. I was never off the bike, and soon got the hang of riding it. I had never felt so free.

Then ,bang , I was on the floor. I had pulled the wrong brake, and went over the handlebars, my knee hurt so much. The brake handle had gone into the side of my right knee. I picked up the bike, and hobbled home, with blood pouring down my leg.

Living in Hope

Some how I got home, and my Foster Mum ,at first , told me off for falling off the bike. When she saw my leg ,she was very sorry for shouting at me. She had thought I had just scraped my knee She took me to the doctor who cleaned the wound, and dressed it. I saw the doctor for the next few weeks. I went back to school with a limp, which disappeared over a period of time, and then I could ride the bike again. No one was going to take away the freedom I felt when I was riding the bike. A part from moving between homes I had always walked every where.

One night my foster parents both had to work, my Foster Mum told me to bath Alice and put her to bed while they were at work. While I was bathing Alice, I asked her to stand still, while I got a towel, but Alice slipped and caught her back on the taps. Alice was really upset and there was a red mark on her back. She would not stop crying.

When my Foster Mum came home, I told her what had happened. I was hit over and over again. Never before had anyone laid a finger on me.

The Social Worker came on her usual visit. She asked me if we were happy. I said yes except for what happened when I was hit for letting Alice fall in the bath. She asked me what had happened, I told her and she took Alice to one side and asked her the same. Alice confirmed what I had said.

I did not know that we were not allowed to stay on our own as we were under age, and on no account should I have been left to bath a younger child.

A couple of days later, the original lady who had taken us to Queensferry, arrived and said she was taking me to another home called Minster lodge, in Ormskirk Lancs.

I was on the move again, on my own.

Shortly afterwards, Alice was taken to Bootle, Liverpool, to new foster parents, on her own.

CHAPTER 4
MINSTER LODGE, ORMSKIRK, LANCS.

5th November 1949 to 22nd December 1949

Once again, I ended up in another home. This time, in a children's home called Minster Lodge, in Ormskirk, Lancashire. From the outside, it looked nice ,a very big house with beautiful gardens and large lawns, with a driveway which went from one gate to the front door, and then out to another gate

I wondered how long I would be here.

The Social worker and I went inside, where we were shown into a very large room to the left of the main door. I noticed that as we looked straight ahead, there was a beautiful staircase with a very big window. I walked into the room, and all the children stopped and looked at me.

I was on my own again.

I broke down and sobbed my heart out, but no one seemed to care. The matron told the lady who had taken me that the more I cried, the quicker I would get over it I thought," how do you get over being taken away from your family? How can you forget?"

I was the kid on the outside again.

The matron came in, and spoke to the Social worker, and then told me that I would soon settle in, and then walked off with the Social worker.

I felt so strange, and so alone. All I wanted was for mum to walk in, put her arms around me, and say that every thing was going to be all right, and take me home, but I knew that was never going to be.

I felt that I was going further and further away from Ramsbottom and my family.

Day after day they were all I thought about.

What kind off life were they having?

Were they being looked after?

Were they loved, after all they were still only babies them selves?

Every day I prayed for the Lord to keep them safe.

At the lodge, I would not allow myself to get close to any one. I stayed on my own. No one will ever hurt me again, never.

I started school yet again after a few weeks, at Cross Hall High school.

This was my fifth school, and I could not settle down. I was so far behind in my education that I could not join in any debates, I did not know what they were talking about.

I thought back to the days at St, Paul's school, where I had been humiliated because I could not write a capital (B). I thought I was right, and wrote it both ways, but the teacher still was not happy. I still think of it to this day.

Living in Hope

At the lodge, when school was over, I would walk back across the fields, looking at the different colours of the trees and bushes. When we arrived at the lodge, we changed out of our school uniform to have our meal..

On Saturday we would walk down Ruff lane, to the post office to put our two shillings and six pence pocket money in to our savings bank.

As it was now autumn, I loved going into the garden to try to brush up the leaves in to little piles, and then watch as the wind blew them away again.

I felt safe to be on my own, doing my own thing.

Matron tried to get me to mix with the other children but I would not—what was the point? I would not be here long. I always get moved on at some time or another.

For so long, I had hoped, and prayed, that I would be going back to my home on the moor, to the chapel school, and seeing the ducks on the pond ,and sitting by the waterfall—remembering my time in Ramsbottom with Auntie Alice, and my grandparents who I loved so very much.

It was never to be, I never saw my mum and dad again.

I never knew if mum loved us, and had she ever loved us, this I will never know.

Just before Christmas 1949, matron called me into her office, and told me of a family in Bootle, Liverpool who would like me to stay with them for Christmas. They had a daughter of similar age to me, and four sons.

My first reaction was to say no, but matron said to give it a try.

On the 22 nd of December1949, I started out for Liverpool with a Social Worker.On the way down, I looked for land marks, as I had done going to Queensferry, and Kirkham, so that I could remember them on my way back.

CHAPTER 5
BOOTLE, LIVERPOOL

22nd December 1949. To Present Day

On the move again, this time to a place called Bootle, on the outskirts of Liverpool

I seemed to be going further and further away from my family. My thoughts were brought to a sudden halt, when I was told we had arrived at the place where I would be spending Christmas

We went into a shop, and a lady came over and said, "You must be Margaret, who has come to stay for Christmas". She told me her name was Mrs Dean. We were invited into another room and met her husband Mr Dean and their daughter Lilian and two sons Ronnie and Keith.

Mrs Dean asked Lilian to show me to where I would be sleeping, as she wanted to talk to the lady who had taken me.

We went up stairs and into a bedroom with two beds. Lilian said I would be in the bed furthest from the door. So I put my small bag of clothes on the bed, then we went back down stairs.

Mrs Dean told me the lady was leaving. We saw her to her car, I said good-by and off she went saying that she would see me after Christmas.

I felt so alone again, another place, and more people to get used to, just for a couple of days.

Later that day I met Harry and Norman who were Mrs Deans other two sons, who had called in before going to their own homes and families

I learned later that the four sons worked on the buses as drivers and were nicknamed the (Dean boys).

They all made me feel very welcome. They were a really nice family. Mr and Mrs Dean asked me did I think I would like it here I said "Yes".

As we walked back into the kitchen, Lilian asked me did I like dogs. She then showed me their dog called Rover. He was sitting on a chair by the fire place.

They also had a very small dog, called Tilley, a Yorkshire terrier. It was the first time I had been any where, where there had been pets.

Bed time came but I could not sleep. The thoughts of my family were never far away.

Where are they now?

Each night I Prayed to God that one day we would all. Meet again.

The day before Christmas, Mrs Dean asked me if I would like to have my hair done for Christmas. She asked Mrs Simpson, the lady who did the house work, to take me through to the shop, and ask one of the staff if they would do my hair.

I had not realized that this was Mrs Deans own shop. I then started to get my hair washed and cut.

Lilian had her hair done as well. Where Lilian was blonde, I was very dark

The shop was very busy, and one of the Ladies asked who I was. Mrs Dean told her I was visiting for Christmas.

Later Lilian took me round to meet her friends. Some of the children had roller skates, including Lilian; who was very good on them. She had no fear. As I had never had a pair of skates before Lilian let me have a go on hers, but I was more on the floor, than on my feet.

It was so strange here, no green fields or moor land to play in. I sat on a wall and thought of my Grandparents garden, and the woodland, where all the children played,

Every where had been so peaceful and quiet , not like here where the noise of the buses and cars going passed all day, was something I had not been used to.

After Christmas I would be off to another home, I thought, as the lady who had brought me, would be back for me after Christmas.

Christmas Eve came, and everyone was busy. All the Dean family would be coming down the next day, for Christmas lunch.

Lilian and I were asked to make mince pies. Mrs Dean showed us what to do, and went back into the shop. I could not believe it. I had never done anything like this before back home. Auntie Alice had always done the baking. I can not remember Mum ever making cakes for us. Lilian kept an eye on me, telling me what to do, as she had made cakes with her mum many times before.

Christmas day arrived and Mrs Dean laid a large table for all the family to sit around. Harry and his wife Elsie with their daughter Sandra and their baby Keith, came early, followed by Norman and his wife Betty, then Ronnie with his girl friend Eleanor, and last but not least Keith, who was not married. I looked across the table at this happy family.

I started to think of my family, and fought to keep back the tears.

I wondered if they had been found nice families for Christmas.

I thought of Mum and Dad and all the Christmases before.

All I remember is having holidays from school. There were no celebrations and I never got any toys.

My thoughts were miles away; they were back home with my family.

I heard someone mention my name, and I was handed a present. I did not know what to do, as I had no presents to give.

Mrs Dean must have noticed me, and saw that I was upset. She said not to worry, just enjoy the day.

We all finished our lunch and the grown ups had coffee. Lilian and I went into another room with Sandra.

Living in Hope

On Boxing Day, there was a party in the evening, for all the family and friends. Every one enjoyed them selves. We did not get to bed till very late.

When Christmas was over, I was waiting for the lady to come and collect me. When she arrived, she had a long talk to Mr and Mrs Dean. She then called me to one side, and asked if I had enjoyed my self. I said," Yes, I had had a good time".

She said Mr and Mrs Dean would like me to stay, for as long as I liked.

Lilian came in, and told me she already knew I was going to be asked to stay, as her Mum and Dad had asked her if she would like me to stay. This was to be the first time I had felt as though I belonged any where. I did not mind if I was not loved as long as someone cared about me.

When Lilian went back to school after Christmas Mrs Dean took me along to see the head mistress and a week or so later, I started at Robert Drive school, the same school as Lilian. I met a lot of Lillian's friends on the first day. Everyone laughed when they heard my Lancashire accent. They kept asking me to say different words, as I pronounced them "funny".

As time went by I started Ballet and Tap, with a Miss Butler, who had a studio near to Stanley Road Bridge. I also took up Piano Lessons, with a Miss Brennan, in Mary Road,.Bootle.

My life had changed so much since I had arrived.

I felt that God had given me a second chance. I had been so poor when I lived in Ramsbottom with no clothes and very little food.

I had come into a life where I had every thing, except my family. After a couple of weeks, Mrs Dean mentioned that we were going away for the weekend, to Wales, and that we had to pack a change of clothes.

On the Friday night, we all got in the car and away we went, through a long tunnel called the Mersey Tunnel.

As we travelled along, I noticed a picture house, which looked familiar. Then I realized it was where Mr and Mrs H my previous foster parents had worked in Queensferry. I did not say any thing I just looked. I got a funny feeling in my stomach thinking of the time I had spent there

Lilian said we did not have far to go now. Half an hour later, we came to a town called Denbigh, in the heart of the country. Then through the country to a lovely cottage, called Ty-isa, with a little stream running along side.

We took the food, and clothes inside, and then Lilian showed me around. There was an orchard at the back, with apple and plum trees. In the corner of the garden, a hammock with lilac trees all around. I thought how lovely it would look in the summer.

Lilian and I were asked to fetch water for the tea. We had to walk down a lane, climb over a fence, and get the water from a well surrounded by trees. We then started

Living in Hope

the walk back up the lane. By the time we got back to the cottage, the buckets where half empty.

How like my home on the moor this place was. It had no electricity, gas or water, the cooking was done by a calor gas cooker and only had three rooms and a kitchen. As it was getting dark, Mr Dean lit oil filled lamps.

We went to stay at Ty- Isa, quite a lot over the next few years.

Then we moved to another cottage, on the side of a farm, called Rossa Fawr. It was much bigger, and had an attic which had Bats, (no way would I ever go up there). As we walked through the farm yard, I noticed a small waterfall with a stream, and as we walked on, there were fields with lots of cows and sheep. How lovely it was here, Lilian and I would spend lots of time playing in the hay stacks during the summer holidays, and helping Bob the farmer This was going to be my life from now on.

As I was growing up, during the school holidays I would be spending a lot of my time here with Mr Dean.

I remember one time during the winter, when we had a snow storm over night. When we tried to open the door, the next morning, we were snowed in, and had to wait for Bob the farmer to dig us out.

I was to find out that Mr Dean had a serious accident on Scotland road, (a main road into Liverpool), when the bus he was driving, swerved to miss a child who had run in front of him. The bus finished up going through the front window of a shop called Breen's, near to where the Wallasey Tunnel is now. As a result Mr Dean suffered serious injuries to his chest and back, and was left having black outs for the rest of his life.

When Mr Dean and I were in Wales on our own, Mr Dean had quite a few blackouts, and as I was only 12, it was very frightening, but I soon got used to them. He would fall on the floor, and I would have to wait until he came round.

At night time, Mr Dean would put a hot brick wrapped up in a towel in my bed, to get it warm. It was so cosy at night time. Mr Dean showed me how to make rugs out of wool, and during the day, we went out and collected wood to make rustic fencing. We found a lot to do up there.

During the summer holidays, Lilian and I would help Bob the farmer, with hay making and milking the cows. In the field opposite the cottage lay a big tree trunk, where most weekends, the family would gather for picnics. About twenty in all. We always finished off with a game of rounders for the children.

As time went by, my foster parents asked me to call them Uncle Alf, and Auntie Nancy. It was so hard to adjust to my new life, when I still had a family of my own.

Not knowing where or what they were doing.

Were they still in care?

Had they been found a nice home, with people who really loved them?

What kind of life had they found?

I still missed them all, so very much.

I never talked about them, as I did not want my foster parents to think I was ungrateful, for giving me a home.

Time went on and suddenly, out of the blue, I received a letter from my brother Hugh. He was stationed in Germany, with the Army, doing his National Service.

I just could not believe it,

He had not forgotten me.

I had always feared that as time went on, my family would not remember me, but Hugh had proved me wrong.

I just cried.

Lilian asked me what was wrong.

I showed her the letter.

She was so excited for me, that she got hold of me and cried. She was so thrilled for me.

I replied back to Hugh, but got no reply. We had moved from Stanley road to Trinity road and during the move Hugh's letter had gone missing and neither of us had each others address That was the last time I would hear from him for a very long time

Lilian and I joined a club called Auntie Margaret's corner, which was part of the Bootle Times Newspaper, and as members, we were invited to a ball, at Bootle Town hall. Once again Auntie Nancy bought the evening dresses. But a couple of days before we were due to go, Lilian fell ill. She was very sick. She had contacted a form of Meningitis, and could have died, but she pulled through. She was very lucky, although it did leave her covered in cold sores all over her face

The time came for Lilian to leave school and become a hairdresser like her Mum

When I was fourteen years old, my best friend Lorna died of a serious illness. Her parents asked if I would like to see her. I said yes. The following day I called at their home and was shown into the front room where Lorna was laid in her coffin. She was all in white, with one single red rose in her hand. Lorna had really jet black hair, and reminded me of Sleeping Beauty. I will never forget how peaceful she looked, but I felt so sad for her parents, as they had lost their only child,

I was starting to make friends of my own, but once again when I got too close to people, I lost them.

Twelve months later, I left school. Although I had always wanted to become a nurse, my changing schools in the early days meant I did not have the education I needed to become a nurse. When I started to think about it, my nerves would always let me down. This was going to stay with me all my life.

I started working in Johnson's cleaners and dyers; I played tennis, and partnered Sands, Sir Tom Johnson's son. We played in mixed doubles matches every weekend, Auntie Nancy bought all my tennis clothes, and rackets for me. And a small case to put all my things in, (which I still have to this day)

In the winter, I played hockey for the team. I had joined the Sports and Social club which had large grounds opposite the factory in Litherland.

Living in Hope

I joined a youth club at Linacre Mission, where I played Badminton, and became a member of the Methodist youth club, and as we where going home from the club one night, Lilian asked our friend Dot and I to go the fair ground, which had arrived at the North Park I said no as we were not allowed, but as I couldn't go home on my own I went along. As we were getting on the waltzer, the car went over my foot. I could hardly walk, but Lilian said try not to limp, During that night I could not sleep for the pain, next morning Auntie Nancy asked what was wrong with my foot , I told her, we ended up at Stanley Hospital, my foot had a bad infection, I was to attend Hospital for the next few weeks. Auntie Nancy said you always get found out when you do things you shouldn't. I was terrified of being sent back to the Children's home,, because I had defied her, I never did it again.

Come the next weekend we went to Wales as usual. Just before we were due to leave for home Auntie Nancy fell, and broke her ankle

She was taken to hospital, and a cast was applied, this she had on for six weeks and then it was taken off, but she still complained of pains in her leg, and was told by the specialist that she had Polio.

She was admitted to hospital, and. While in there, Auntie Nancy got pleurisy. We were told there was only a fifty chance of recovery.

I thank God she pulled through.

In the meantime, we had moved from the hairdressers, to a house in Trinity Road Bootle. It was a big house and Auntie Nancy had a bed brought down stairs. It was put in the lounge, so she could look out over the lovely garden. It had six bed rooms, four rooms down stairs, and a basement with a large games room.

During one of our holidays, we went to Brighton. Auntie Nancy suggested we have a picnic, so we found a little bakers shop. As Auntie Nancy was in her wheel chair, Uncle Alf stayed out side with her. The shop smelled lovely. The bread was still hot. Auntie Nancy asked Lilian and me to get some currant buns, with the bread. This we did, and put it all on Auntie Nancy's knee.

We started to cross a road that was very busy. The buns dropped off Auntie Nancy's knee and scattered all over the road. Uncle Alf told us to "get the buns" ⊠ bearing in mind this road was very busy,) Lilian and I were sent dashing in and out of the traffic, to pick up the buns. The car drivers were hooting their car horns at us ,but Uncle Alf just said to get the buns How the cars missed us I will never know. We got them all, not one bun had a tyre mark on it.

.I received a letter from my Auntie Alice, with two photographs, of my brothers James and John.

I went to my room, and cried.

Why? If Auntie Alice knew where I was, did she never come and see me. Or make some kind of contact. I put those pictures away, but I looked at them every day, wondering how John and James were, and what they

Living in Hope

had grown up like, and what they had been like as small children. Our entire child hood had been taken away from us, and I will never forgive the people who did it. They destroyed my family.

When I was seventeen I started going to Litherland Town hall with my friend Dot, who I had met while working in Johnson's, and also at Linacre Mission. We became and still are very good friends.

It was at the town hall that I met Tom, who was to become my husband, and Dot met Bob who was the image of Tony Curtis and later married him. Lilian came with me one night to the Town Hall, and while we were there, she met a tall, good looking, sunburnt chap. His name was Freddie, he was a seaman, but was home on leave. They started going out, and later married at St, Andrews church Bootle on the 3rd of October 1959, both Dot and I and our niece Sandra were bridesmaids, Lilian and Freddie had two sons Stephen and David, and two daughters, Christine and Janet. They had four grand children, Lean, Robert, Thomas, and Keith. Lilian lost her husband due to cancer. She nursed him at home, for sometime, and did an excellent job, but it was not to be; Freddie died at the age of fifty eight years of age. Lilian was devastated, but she had four good children to help her through.

Tom and I were married at Christ Church Bootle on March 5th 1960. Lilian, Dot, and Sandra were my bridesmaids. The vicar asked Tom and I, if I would consider walking into church to some thing different, as he had always wanted a change from the traditional, "here comes the bride" We said we would oblige, as he was retiring after our wedding, and it would be the last wedding ceremony he would conduct we decided on "Guide me o thou great Redeemer".

It was a couple of months later, when Princess Margaret got married, that the Royal couple did the same thing. Just before we got married, Auntie Nancy asked would we like to stay with her and Uncle Alf, as the house was too big for the two of them. We said that if they did not mind, we would like to start out on our own. So Auntie Nancy and Uncle Alf moved back to the cottage in Wales, back to their family roots, and I went to stay with Harry and Elsie, Sandra, and Keith.

When we got married Tom and I moved into a flat in Waterloo, and were there for twelve months, when we moved into a house in Watling Avenue, Litherland on the twenty second of December 1961. I was four months pregnant, and we wanted to get the living room decorated for Christmas. Toms Mum and Dad helped us. My sister in law Elsie had invited us up to their house on Christmas day but instead I ended up in hospital with a miscarriage I lost my baby on Christmas day.

In 1962, I had a little girl who we later christened Gaynor, in Walton hospital; (it was at this time that Tom's sister Pat started dating Tom's friend Norman. We have always said it was Gaynor that brought them together).

I had been for a routine check up, with my doctor, as I had not been feeling well. The doctor told me that I

Living in Hope

had to go into hospital immediately, as I had high blood pressure. While I was in Walton hospital, a young nurse told me that Gaynor had had a blood change.

I just sat and cried.

Why hadn't I been told before it was done, after all I was her Mum

When Tom and Auntie Nancy came, I told them what the nurse had said. Tom asked to see the matron, and she went to see what was happening. When she came back, she gave me her word that Gaynor was fine, and had definitely not had her blood changed. In fact Gaynor had Yellow Jaundice and fluid on the lungs, and this was the reason for her being in an incubator

Of the two weeks in hospital, it was only for the last three days that I was able to see and nurse Gaynor. Every time Tom had visited, I had insisted that he went down to the nursery to check on Gaynor. I had a horrible feeling that something had happened to her.

The day before I came out of hospital Auntie Nancy asked me to call her Mum. I don't know why, but I said I could not, as I already had a Mum,

Even though I did not know where she was. I still held her close in my heart.

When I finally came home with Gaynor, it was the happiest time of my life. I would give her all the love I could give. Toms Granddad came to see her, and held a five pound note (the old big white five pound note)

He asked what we were going to call her. We told him her name would be Gaynor. He said that the eldest girl in each generation had to be called Blanche, and had been for many Generations. In a similar way the boys, had always been called Thomas Joseph (as was Tom my husband)

I had broken the tradition. (He instantly put the five pound back in his pocket, and gave Gaynor a one pound note).

We bought her a high pram, and beautiful clothes. As she got older, we bought her clothes from Chester, she always looked lovely.

When Gaynor was a baby, we travelled up to Wales every weekend, to see Auntie Nancy and Uncle Alf. We did not want Gaynor missing out, by not having her grandparents. We would go by train, and Uncle Alf would meet us in Mold, and take us the rest of the way by car. Gaynor spent most of her baby weekends in Wales. One weekend we went to a dance in the North Wales Mental Hospital, the band was Johnny Dankworth and lead singer Cleo Laine, his newly married wife. During the night, we were doing the conga, and for some reason, we all ended up in a padded cell down one of the corridors, and got locked in. We were there for some time, before we were missed. Some one had seen us heading in that direction and came to look for us. They could see we were not inmates as we were all in evening wear.

We went up as usual the following weekend, and went down to Denbigh market with Auntie Nancy, but this time she did not want to take her walking stick. She walked unaided. We had a lovely day, and when we

Living in Hope

had finished the shopping, we went back home to the cottage.

Auntie Nancy said she wished we could stay, but we had to come home for Tom to go to work. As we were leaving she got upset, and asked me to stay, but I said I would phone when we got home. As promised we rang, Uncle Alf said Auntie Nancy was taking a bath, and would tell her we had phoned.

During that night we were woken up by our Ronnie, to tell us Auntie Nancy had collapsed in the arms of Uncle Alf, when she was getting out of the bath, and had died. I think she knew some thing was wrong, when she asked me to stay.

After telling my self never to get too close to anyone again, it was fateful, it was happening all over again.

No mother figure to turn to.

I felt an awful emptiness inside.

As soon as we could we all went up to Wales, to be with Uncle Alf. He was devastated.

Tom took the day off work to look after Gaynor, while I went with my foster family.

Auntie Nancy was brought back to Liverpool to be cremated and her ashes were then taken back to Wales.

Not long after, Uncle Alf went to live with his son Harry, because his health had started to fail. He had been found collapsed, in a field, while he was walking down to Denbigh. A farmer had found him, and had called an ambulance. He was taken to Holywell hospital. We all went up to see him, and decided he could not live on his own. Hence he went to live with Harry.

Then a couple of years later Keith was rushed into Walton hospital, suffering a massive heart attack The night Tom and I went to visit him, he said he wanted to go home to his Mum, for his birthday, 17th March. I said that's not possible, as his Mum had died, but Keith kept on saying it.

At the end of visiting time we left for home, and had not long been in, when the police were knocking on the door, to say that Keith had just passed away. We just could not believe it, but he got his wish. He had gone home to his Mum.

I was starting to lose the people who had given me a home, for the ten years before I got married, and had the feeling I was starting to lose yet another family.

When it was time for Gaynor to start school we had another little girl, Suzanne,.I went into hospital and into the same ward, and the same bed space as I had been when Gaynor was born. Again I was in for two weeks. Fortunately Suzanne's birth was straight forward without any complications

We had already picked the pram for Sue, a lovely navy and white, and had also picked a dolls pram in the same colours for Gaynor, so that she would not feel pushed out. I felt so proud taking Suzanne out in her pram, with Gaynor walking along side, pushing her dolls pram.

Living in Hope

As Sue grew older she had dark waist length hair and like Gaynor always beautifully dressed. Where Sue was dark like me, Gaynor was fair like her dad.

When Sue started school I felt so lost. As for the last ten years I had been occupied looking after my girls. The Teacher asked me if I was going to get a job I said no, so she asked if I would like to help in school. So I did, taking the children for reading and helping with their swimming lessons. I loved every minute I was there and ended up doing voluntary work for five years, I was offered a job on school dinners, which I did for some time.

Tom was working at English Electric as a Quality Control Engineer. Every thing was going well.

I was happily married, with two daughters, a nice house, and Tom had a good job.

Then we had a big shock:-

English Electric was moving from Liverpool to Stafford and there was going to be massive redundancies.

Tom was made redundant, there was going to be hard times ahead. No wages would be coming in, so we would have to cut back

I started Mabel Fletcher College to get some training. I had always wanted to be a nurse, so I thought I would go in for the care side of work

When I finished college I was a qualified care assistant and went to work in Alder Hey Children's Hospital as an Auxiliary Nurse. I worked on ward B 3 with a sister called Jenny, who I got on very well with. I stayed there for a few years working mainly evenings. There was no way that our two girls were ever to be left

I was there for the girls during the day, and Tom was there in the evening.

Tom had a few different jobs, and finally settled down at Skil Controls Skelmersdale where he became a manager.

It appeared things were looking up again

Where Gaynor had gone to ballet and tap, Sue had started Ice –skating. They both did very well in there chosen activities.

Then Tom's Dad was taken ill with cancer of the prostrate.

I left work to help Tom's Mum look after his Dad. He was ill for sometime, at home, and was looked after by his family. I spent a lot of time with Tom's Dad. Tom's Mum and I would walk Dad around the bedroom to keep his circulation going. We used to have a laugh, he would always head for the door, hoping to get down stairs, but I had to say, "no, not to-day, maybe tomorrow".

Tomorrow never came, he became confined to bed, and slowly sank into a coma. All we could do was make him comfortable. The Macmillan nurses came every day to wash him,

Tom's Dad died in the early spring of 1984.

After two years of living on her own, Tom's Mum moved into sheltered accommodation, and was only there a week when she died of a massive heart, attack just before our Sue's 18th birthday.

Living in Hope

Gaynor met Neville, while they were training to be nurses at Walton Hospital. They married two years later, and 11 years later had a daughter Aimee. Sue met and married Ian, and had a daughter called Gemma. Sue divorced Ian, and has now met Kevin, both Gaynor and Sue live within easy walking distance of us.

With our two girls married, we then had time on our hands , (unless baby sitting) and saw Ronnie and Eleanor at the weekends. The four of us decided to have a holiday together, and travel by coach, to Holland and Germany. We had some lovely times together.

. Then Ronnie took ill with cancer and had to be fed by tube. I would go every morning to take his newspaper, and then every afternoon, when I finished work, to give Eleanor a break, just while she went to the shops. Ronnie only lived for five months after being diagnosed. It was an awful shock to every one.

I remember Ronnie saying, that when he got well, we would go back to Holland, only this time we would go by car, with Tom and Ronnie sharing the driving. We would stay bed and breakfast, so we could please our selves where we stayed.

It was not to be, Ronnie died in the October just before his birthday.

Five years ago, Sue, Gemma and Kev were involved in a car crash. A motor bike came round the corner on the wrong side of the road. It was a head on collision; the biker admitted it was his fault, in court. Sue has had to finish work, as it has left her left leg with bad injuries. She suffers 24 hours a day. Gaynor also had a car crash. Again not her fault, and suffers pain in her neck and arms.

I pray that if I could take away their pain, I would.

It hurts so much to see them suffer, I love them so much.

I have always tried to give my two girls, the things I never had. We did not always have the money to spend on them, but I hope I am giving them all the love I never had

When I visit Ramsbottom, I go to the cemetery ,where my Mum is buried to tend her grave. I start to think back to when I went with Mum to my Grandparents grave. I remember how lonely she had looked then. As when I put flowers on my Mums grave, even though I never had my Mum for all those years, I still feel a terrible sense of loss. I miss her so much, I never had the chance to say good by, even though I was 11 years old when I last saw her, I had hoped that if, and when I found my family, I would see my Mum.

It is said that time heals and takes away the heartache but for some people It never goes away. When on my own, I think about my home on the moor and how happy we were, I still shed tears for all those lost years with out my beloved family

CHAPTER 6
THE HUNT FOR MY FAMILY

I was on my way to pick Tom (my husband) up from work. I asked our Sue (our daughter) and Gemma (our grand daughter) if they wanted to come for the ride. As we were going along the motorway, to Skelmersdale, Sue asked me why my name was different from that of the Dean family. I then told her about my life before I came to Liverpool.

She could not believe, that during all those years, I had never spoken of my real family. But as I said to her, even though I never mentioned them, they were never out of my thoughts, and always in my heart.

One day, God willing, when the time was right, I would see them again.

The next day, Sue asked me if I would like to try and find my family. I was hesitant at first, because over the years, Tom and I had often been through Ramsbottom and Bury. As we had driven through the little town, where I was born, I had seen the little shop, where I used to get my ice-cream, and remembered where my Grandparents house was. All those memories came flooding back.

But as I had never spoken of my family, I kept my thoughts to my self. Tom had often asked me what had happened, but he had accepted that I did not want to talk about it.

After we had picked Tom up, the journey back home was very quiet, my thoughts were elsewhere. Over the years I had wanted to find my family, but as I have said before, I did not want to hurt my foster parents as they had given me a home and cared for me when no-one else did.

With all my family involved we began the hunt.

"What if they did not remember me, or simply did not want to know"? All these thoughts were going on in my mind.

The thought of seeing them all again, after 56 years, -----Mums first reaction, -----and that of the rest of the family, made me feel very apprehensive. But I decided to try and trace my roots.

Sue tried the internet, with out success. So Tom and I went over to the library at the Civic Hall in Crosby, and looked through all the Merseyside Telephone Directories, and listed all the names of Grundy with their phone numbers, (I had mentioned to Tom, that some years ago, Auntie Nancy had told me, that my sister Alice had had her name changed from Alice Russell to Alice Russell-Grundy).

As it was time for the Civic Hall to close, we came home. We went through all the names Grundy, that lived in Bootle, we phoned every one up, with out success. Our Gemma, said to try further a field, as she may have

Living in Hope

moved. This we did, and found a number, which turned out to be a relation of Alice...

She said Alice had married, and they had lost touch with each other, but she gave us a telephone number in Colwyn Bay, North Wales, which was her cousin, who had kept in touch with her.

At last, someone who knew where Alice lived. The cousin gave us Alice's phone number as she had moved to Nottingham.

As Tom had to go to work the next day, I asked our Sue to ring for me, my nerves had gone. Sue phoned the number and a man answered. He said he was Alice's husband Bill, and that he would tell Alice when she came home.

That day, I spoke to my sister, for the first time since we had parted at the end of 1949. when we had left our foster parents in Queensferry and had lost touch until I moved to Liverpool. Some how Alice found me, and came to visit, but it was not to last. One of the foster mums did not agree to us seeing each other; for what reason we would never know. It was tears on both ends of the phone. We spoke for what seemed hours, we had a lot of catching up to do. The two daughters had found each other again

Alice told me that she knew where John lived, and gave us his phone number.

The next day, we phoned and I spoke to my brother John. He was just two years old, when I had last seen him. He told me that Stephen had traced Alice and him some years ago. After talking to John on the phone, he phoned Stephen, and told him that I had been found, and gave him my phone number.

Later on John got in touch with our Sue, and said he was going to come down and surprise me.

That Saturday, I was out in the front garden with my granddaughter, Aimee. I looked down the road, and a man and woman were walking up. He looked familiar. As they got nearer, I heard him say that's our Margaret, doing the garden. I just froze; it was my brother John, and his wife Barbara. It was hugs and kisses, and might I say tears of joy.

The last time I saw John, was when he was waving me off to school 56 years ago. I just did not want to let him go. I had carried his photograph all these years, wondering what he would look like, and what kind of life he had lived. Now I know, John can not remember any thing about what happened, as he was only three years of age, but was told that he had a family some where. John had been trying for years to find me but it was me who found him. John had given up some years ago but he had managed to find Alice , Hugh, Stephen.

After John and Barbara had gone, I had a phone call from my baby brother Stephen.

The surprise I got when Stephen phoned me was unbelievable. He was just five months old when I last saw him. I was talking to my baby brother, after 56years. He told me that he had been trying to trace me since 1973, but could not find where I had moved to, when

Living in Hope

we had moved from the hair dressers. He had contacted Radio Merseyside but without any luck, and had put a piece in the Liverpool Echo, again without any luck. He said that every way he tried, he came up against a brick wall, and at one stage, thought he would never find me. He had recently been thinking of contacting Cilla Black, on Surprise Surprise, but as he said, now we can stop watching Surprise Surprise.

After hearing from Stephen, things happened so quickly, I just could not take it in, now there was Hugh and James to find..

As a result of the feature appearing in the Bury Times, we were inundated with telephone calls. One call was from a girl called Karen. She said her father had mentioned that he met a chap, every Thursday in a coffee shop at the Bury Interchange and that his name was Hugh. She said that she would phone us back the following week, with any more details she could find out from her Dad. She phoned us back a week later, and said the chaps name was Hugh Russell.

A few days later, we went up to Bury, with a bunch of flowers for Miss Choudrey, who had helped me so much to get this hunt started. We mentioned about Hugh.

A few minutes later, she returned from her office, and said that a man named Hugh Russell did live in Knight Street, and also gave us the house number, telephone number and a map on how to get there from her office.

The following morning, we decided that Tom would phone Hugh, and he found it was my brother Hugh, and past the phone over to me. I had found my eldest brother.

Up to this point, I had found three brothers, and my Sister.

Only one brother had to be found.

We all decided to have a reunion, in Ramsbottom, at the Rose and Crown. John and his wife Barbara, Tom and I, went up to Ramsbottom, and made the arrangement, we picked the 3rd of November.

All we had to do was to find James. We all tried ringing a number we had found in the Yorkshire Directory, but we kept getting the unobtainable tone. John's daughter Judith tried the internet, and found an address in Todmorden. So they decided to go up in their car rather than phone. They had not mentioned it to anyone, in case it wasn't James.

Sue and I had gone shopping, and when we arrived back, Gemma was shouting for us to hurry up.

She said Uncle John was on the telephone.

I had a strange feeling, and I said to Sue, I think they have found James.

John asked me to sit down, as he had some news for me. I said," Have you found James?" he said "yes".

James had changed his telephone number the week before, and that's why we could not get a reply from the number, we had all been trying. We traced James on the 19th of October, his Birthday. What a day it was, A dream come true from all those years ago, when I had told him,

Living in Hope

I would not be long, and that turned out to be 56 years later, My Prayers had been answered.

November 3rd came and I had had a cake made at David's in Crosby, the people who make cakes for the Royal Family. I walked into the Rose and Crown and there standing at the bar, was my brother James. I thought I had shed all the tears I had but when I saw James the tears just flowed.

> My brother Hugh was the only one who could not make it, as he was too ill to attend.

I was to find out that Stephen Hugh Alice John had traced Mum some years earlier. John showed me where her grave was.

I was never to see my Mum and Dad again.

Mum died in 1981 aged 67 and Dad died in 1960 aged 53,

People say that time heals, I still shed tears from all those lost years with out my beloved family, who for 56 years, I Prayed that when the time was right, I would find them all again.

I believe that God has a plan for every one, for when Hugh needed help, Tom, James, Sandra and I were there, and his nieces Gaynor, Sue, Gemma and his little Aimee.

Chapter 7
Dad

Where were you, and why?

During my growing up years Dad seemed to be here one day , gone the next , never knowing where to ,I remember Granddad talking about the war. Had Dad joined the army, for the war? I never knew. Until I had found my brothers and sister a few years earlier I realized I had more searching to do to find out about my Dad and would not rest until I had

Going on the address on Dads Death Certificate, (9 Zion Street Bacup), we decided to try the Library for census forms, but nothing was found. We then picked up the person who had registered Dads Death. It was a Mr William Oliver ,brother –in- law. We found his address in Burnley But unfortunatley he had died and we could not find any other details not knowing which of Dads family he had married.

Talking to different people , we were given the address of a gentleman, whose name was Mr Walsh. He had lived in Bacup all his life, and may know some one who may have known dad. Giving it a try we called to see Mr Walsh,(pressing the wrong bell 20 instead of 19) we were answered by a Mr Bodie who kindly came down to talk to us and explained that for security reasons they had

Living in Hope

to be careful who they invited in. We explained what we were trying to do.

Mr Bodie (Pete) and his wife Marlene made us a cup of tea when they knew we had travelled from Liverpool, and as we talked Pete asked had we tried the Rossendale Free Press News Paper, Pete said his friend was the editor and gave us her name suggesting that we contact her. After spending most of the afternoon with them we thanked Pete and Marlene for all their help. We then set off home back to Liverpool

The following day we decided a to take a trip up to the Rossendale Free Press News Paper we were introduced to a lady called Jenny, who after hearing our story, decided it would appear in the paper the following week

The paper came out the following Friday. On the Saturday we received a phone call from a lady who said she may be related to me. It turned out that her Mum Maude was my dads sister. After talking for a while Maureen invited us up to visit, she lived in a little place called Waterfoot near Bacup. We arranged to go up the following Thursday Maureen said that when she saw the photograph in the paper thought how like her uncle Hugh I was, she then read the article about me trying to find out about my dad, the name was the same where he died and where he was buried, to much a coincidence she thought so decided to phone me and yes we are related.

On the Sunday we had just arrived back from church, the phone rang , it was another lady saying she thought we could be cousins after exchanging a few details she said she had read the article, her name was Madeline, and she suggested I give her sister a call as she could give me more information about my Dad. She gave me the phone number when I called the first thing she said was," is that our Margaret?" I was speaking to Sheila their Mum turned out be Amy (My Mum and Dads Bridesmaid) (dads other sister).

Tom and I were invited to their house the following week, what a visit that turned out to be, Photographs of my grandparents, my Dad when he was in the army which he Joined in1927, Sheila also mentioned that Dad had served in India during his time in the army. Now I knew the reason why dad had kept disappearing in my early years.

What a day, then to round it all off I was given a photograph of Mum with Hugh my brother when he was four years old and myself when I was three years old, I never knew this photograph existed, imagine my feelings at seeing this for the very first time mum was holding my hand I can not explain how I felt.

During the day I was shown my Grandparents Russells old house and also the grave where they now rest. I now have a much larger family I never knew existed.

Until I had found my Dads family who had read the Rossendale Paper they had never known about the family being split up all those years ago.

This is a message for you Dad,

Living in Hope

"I never got to see you again to tell you how proud I am of you, but I have sent a message to someone very special up there to give it to you personally"

From your loving Daughter
Margaret

CHAPTER 8
REVISITS TO MY PREVIOUS HOMES

During the research which had to be done for this book, Tom, my husband, and I travelled many miles to confirm my memories of the places where I had lived. It was a huge task I had only been 10years old at the time, and in the majority of places I only had a picture in my mind---no names or road names---just an idea of where about it was.

For no particular reason, I thought that probably the best place to start was to find out exactly where we had lived in "Rammy"—as much as I could about my family back ground –and why the six children had been taken into care.

We had often passed through Rammy since we had been married but I had never wanted to stop. Apart from knowing that I was born in Rammy, and was fostered by Mr and Mrs Dean, Tom knew nothing about my past. I had always said that when I felt that it was right I would tell the full story to him.

I felt that then was the right time.

RAMSBOTTOM:-

On our first trip to Rammy we were able to go straight to Union St, where Hugh and I had been born at No 6.

Living in Hope

Unfortunately most of the street was now a part of the Quick Save car park.

We had been given two copies of old photographs of Union St, during a visit to Bury Archives. One photograph had a lady standing in a doorway, which could be our Mum, but we are not completely sure, as we cannot see any numbers on the door, and of all the dozens of maps we have looked at-not one has shown any house numbers. Then there was Brooks Dairy which was opposite our house.

The other photograph looked up Union street towards Prince Street.

We also visited Kenyon Street where Mum and Auntie Alice had worked all those years ago, then up to Fir Street where My Grandparents had lived. All the happy memories came flooding back.

Our next stop was to see where our Auntie Alice had lived, then on to the woodlands where we used to play, I closed my eyes, and could still see and hear the children as they played, my cousins Fred and Jean, and my bothers James and Hugh, and sister Alice, we were all so happy.

As we made our way down Bridge Street, I called into my old school, St Paul, which had not changed at all.

I felt so sad, thinking back to all those years wondering how my life would have turned out if I had stayed in Ramsbottom.

I saw the secretary, and explained what I was looking for. She said she would not be long, and left the office, and after a while she came back, carrying the register from when I had started school. She not only had mine but that of my brother Hugh, and my sister Alice.

These were the only records of me that I had found. Until then I had no proof that I existed before the age of eleven. I was also given some photographs of children who may have been in my class, but I could not remember them. Not knowing what I looked like before the age of eleven (did I have long or short hair) I could not pick one out that might have resembled me at such a young age.

St, Paul Church is still there, but I was to find out that the school was to be pulled down to make way for luxury flats.

After leaving the school, I did what I had always wanted to do as a child, and that was to go inside the church. I walked down to the communion rail, and thought that when finally I did go in, it would have been with my Mum, Dad and family but that will never be.

The tears just started to flow.

I walked back up the aisle, I was approached by a member of the church, and asked if he could be of any help, and not to hesitate with any questions. What he did tell us, was the font had been moved from the back of the church, to the side by the organ.

Ramsbottom its self has not changed. While a few new estates have been built they are all on the outskirts of the old town which is still as I remember it The people up there are still so very friendly, we have made so many friends.

Living in Hope

Last Easter, we went to see if the annual event of egg rolling still went on. To our amazement people still walked to the top of Peel Tower. As we arrived, a church service was going on, in a crevice on the hillside. People were playing guitars and singing hymns, the atmosphere was amazing. As people walked towards the tower, every one was helping each other to get to the top. People were pushing prams to give the mums a rest, and offering to carry the children, it was more like a Pilgrimage than a day out

My grand daughter Aimee could not wait to roll her painted egg, along with all the other children. With out me knowing, Aimee had bought a dummy egg that looked like a real one. As we started to roll the eggs, mine smashed on the first rock that it hit, Aimee, well, her egg just bounced, she had bought a rubber one, talk about cheating,

We all started the walk back down the hill to-wards Holcombe church, then past Auntie Alice's old house in Mount Street.

It was an amazing experience and not commercial-ised.

The memories I had, and have, will never leave me.

Watching Aimee to-day, took me back to when I was her age. Happy and carefree

BUCKHURST:-

All my life, I knew I had to try and find the cottage, where we were so happy and free, and retrace the foot steps that we took all those years ago, with our Mum.

All I could remember was walking up a lane with a very high wall, and then a dirt track, which seemed unending at the time, and eventually arriving at a cottage with a waterfall at the side, which was near to a chapel and a large pond. My brother Hugh had recently told me that it was near to Nangreaves, on the other side of Walmsley Road to Ramsbottom, up on the moors

We tried many side roads, off the main road, but could not find the high wall, or any signs of where there had been one. Many of the "locals" who we asked did not recognise my description of the cottage. Eventually we called at a farm house, and explained what we were looking for. The lady immediately recognised my description, and told us it was by Buckhurst Farm and told us how to get there, in the car.

As we walked down the lane, to the cottage, a man approached us. He asked if he could help as we were on his property. I explained the reason for being there. He told me his name was Mr Ashe and that he and his family lived in the cottage, and invited us down to the cottage. I could hear the sound of children's laughter, and as we got nearer I noticed a girl of about ten years of age, and three other children, Mrs Ashe said she had another baby in the cottage. All the children were the same ages as we had been, when we had lived there all those years ago.

It was like history repeating itself.

Tom could not get over how quiet and peaceful it was up on the moor, as he had always lived in the town.

Living in Hope

Mr Ashe told us that we were welcome to go up there any time. So a few weeks later we took John, James, Alice, Stephen and their families.

We were all back home, where we had all lived, and been so happy.

There were lots of tears, as we shared our memories.

Stephen, of course, was only a few months old when we were up there, and had no memory of the cottage, but was very happy to have found where we had lived when he was born.

John was very similar to Stephen, as he was only 18 months old, but John told us that when he was very young he would always draw a picture of a cottage with trees. He never new why, or where the place was.

James, Alice, and I remembered it very well.

The only one who could not get there was Hugh our eldest brother, who was too ill to travel, but I knew in my heart, that he was there with us.

At this stage, we had found the cottage and taken the rest of the family to see it.

Now I had to try and find the way that we and our Mum had walked up to the cottage. We had used the cars to take the rest of the family up there, which must have been about 4 miles and much too far for Mum to walk with the five children, and also bearing in mind that she was about 8 months pregnant with Stephen.

We took a look at the A-Z, now that we knew where we were trying to get to, and decided to walk up Whitelow Road. The road? was a dirt track made up of small boulders with water running down between the boulders. It was out of the question to go up in the car, but there was a stone wall, which could have looked huge to a 10 year old child (as I had been the last time I had been there.) We decided to carry on and came to Bury Old Road, where we turned right, and walked past Nangreaves.

Our brother Hugh was right. At Snape Hill we picked a foot path to White Wall Farm then onto Salas's Farm on Salas's Lane and then onto the cottage.

It took us about an hour to walk to the cottage, although it would have taken Mum a lot longer with the pram, even if the paths had been a lot better.

Was this the way that Mum walked? I will never know, but I think it is the most likely.

When we arrived at the Chapel, we sat on the bench which is on the side of the narrow road and had a bite to eat. Sitting there, it was so quiet that it almost hurt our ears, then after a while, having been in another world, we had to make a move to get off the moors before dark.

Walking back to the car was down hill all the way, and only took about 45 minutes.

JERICHO:-

Shortly after finding my brother Hugh, he was taken ill and admitted to Fairfield Hospital in Bury. While visiting Hugh, I was asked to make an appointment to meet his Social Worker, called Alistair Mitchell, to discuss

Living in Hope

my brothers care programme. We decided to see Alistair after visiting.

We were directed to a building which housed Alistair's office. We walked through the hospital and out through a door.

Imagine my feelings. In front of us was a long red brick building with a veranda running the full length. Alistair's office was in the same building as Jericho Workhouse had been all those years ago.

I stopped in my tracks. The thought of entering the building made my stomach churn and I felt physically sick. I was remembering the fear and loneliness I had experienced as a child. In my mind, I could still see the white walls, with rows of beds down both sides of the room, and the ladies sitting at the side of their beds, not talking.

I still can not understand why children could be put into a place like this.

Tom had mentioned to Alistair about what had happened to me.

We had found out that the area around the hospital was in fact the district of Jericho, and in a lot of cases the workhouses had become hospitals, but with visiting Hugh, and not getting back to Liverpool until about 9.30 each evening I had just not had time to find the workhouse.

We met Alistair, while I was trying to come to terms with my feelings and as we entered the building, he must have sensed my reaction, even though the building was now converted into small offices. As we walked to his office he kept asking me if I was alright. He was really concerned. When we reached his office we had coffee and just chatted for a while. It was so obvious that he was helping me to overcome what I had just been through

Alistair became a friend of the family, who helped us through the most difficult time when Hugh was so ill.

I will never be able to thank him enough.

KIRKHAM:-

When we decided to see if we could find the children's home in Kirkham, I had to rely completely on my memory once again. Bearing in mind that when I went to Kirkham, it was only a few weeks earlier that I had been taken away from my family and placed in Jericho Workhouse, where later I met up with Alice, James and Hugh only to be moved on again on my own.

How reliable was my memory after all that had happened?

We decided to drive up to Kirkham, which is in between Preston and Blackpool with only a picture in my mind. We did not even know if it was a village or a town, as we had not been allowed out of the home except to go to school or church.

We drove around the town for some time, mainly on the main roads or where there were large houses, and eventually found the Baths. Alongside was a large building being used by Human Resources for Social Services.

Living in Hope

That was the entrance to the home where I had stayed.

We decided to go in and talk to some one, who may be able to help. At Reception, a lady asked if she could be of any help to us, and I explained what we were trying to do. She asked us to wait and went into another office. Not long afterwards, she came back, but could tell us nothing apart from the fact that it had been a children's home some years ago, but had no idea where any records would be held, but did give us some information on a chap who had done a lot of research on the home. We decided to phone him when we got home.

I asked the lady if we could go through to where the children had lived, there was no problem. She showed us through to a back door, and the memories came flooding back, we were walking the same way I had walked when I had first gone to the home. On the way through the offices, the lady asked if I would like to see a door way which had purposely not been modernised. It was unbelievable, dark green wall tiles covered all the walls, and the dark brown door had a large stained glass panel set into it. After my memory being "jogged" again, I wondered why I had not remembered it before.

We went through the back door, and came to the row houses where the children had lived. I had told Tom that I had been in No7, and as we came out of the door I pointed out the actual house, then as we got nearer we realised that it was No7, and again had been converted into offices. The playground was now a car park.

In a way it was a bit disappointing, I suppose I was hoping that nothing had changed, and I could have gone into No7, and seen some children in there.

We came away, and decided to try and find the school, so far I still had no written proof that I had ever been there.

As we came out on to the main road we turned left, past the baths, looking for the railway bridge, when suddenly, in front of us, was the bridge. I was on my way to school.

We decided to park the car, and walk. The road bent round to the right, and there on the right was my old school.

By this time, it must have been around 3PM, the mums were in the play ground waiting for their children. So we decided to go straight in and saw the receptionist. She told us that she had been there for many years, then took us round the school, explaining the changes that had been made over the years, and then took us back to the office for a coffee. I explained to her what I was trying to do and asked if there were any records held in the school. She said that there were, but she would need permission from the head to show them to me, and as the school was now closed could I phone up the following Monday.

While I was waiting for Monday to arrive, I phoned the researcher who had done all the work on the home. He told me that he had a list of all the children who had been at the home, but the names of my sister and I were not on the list. He was very helpful and sent me a copy

Living in Hope

of the list in case there was a misspelling taken from old documents.

Monday finally came, and I phoned up the school, and the receptionist told me that she had found the register which I would find very interesting, and the head had given his approval for me to see it, but could not discuss it on the phone. We arranged to go to the school the following day.

When we arrived, we were introduced to the head, who asked me to let him know if there was any thing he could do to help me, and left us with the receptionist. She took out the register for new starters, and an entry showing that six children, who were resident at Kirkham Children's Home had started at the school. The names of the six children included myself, my sister Alice, and another girl who I had remembered.

At last I had the proof that I had lived in Kirkham

ORMSKIRK:-

Minster Lodge in Ormskirk is only about 16 miles from where we now live and was easy for us to find. I knew it was in Ruff Lane, but I wanted to know more about it.

We soon found the beautiful, detached house, and parked the car outside the large gates.

We walked up the long drive, which went up to the front of the house and back to another set of gates at the other side of the huge lawn. On both sides of the drive were tall trees, just as I remembered it.

As we approached the front door, a lady came out and asked if she could help us. I explained what I was trying to do, and she invited us inside. I could not believe it. It had not changed very much in all those years. What a difference it was to Jericho and Kirkham which were now office blocks.

The room which I had been shown into, all those years ago, on my arrival, was now a dining room, and the lovely dark wooden staircase, was just as I had remembered it.

All the memories came flooding back. The tears when I fist went in—the loneliness when I would not mix, and the uncertainty when I was told I would be going to Liverpool for Christmas.

I asked the lady, if there were fields at the back of the home, as I used to walk across them to school. She asked me to follow her up the stairs to the first landing, where we saw what was left of the fields –very little and the beautiful trees had gone. In their place is the Ormskirk Hospital A and E Dept.

I mentioned the school that I had attended, and was it still there, she said it was, and pointed us in the direction. We left saying thank you for her time and all the help she had given us.

We followed the directions we had been given, and there was my old school, even if it was only for a short time, it was called Cross Hall High School.

I had re-traced my foot steps at Minster Lodge.

LIVERPOOL:-

There has not been any reason for revisiting as I finally settled down in Liverpool and still live there to this day.

Part 3
Hugh's Story

Written By Margaret

CHAPTER 1

Hugh in 2001 at 1st meeting with Margaret

The first time I found out about Hugh was when a lady called Karen telephoned me at home, from Bury. She had read about me in the Bury Times – where an article had been written asking for help in trying to find my family.

Karen said her father had mentioned that he met a chap every Thursday, in a coffee shop at the Bury Interchange, and that his name was Hugh. She would see her Dad during the week and phone me back with any more details she could get from her Dad.

True to her word, Karen phoned back a week later, and said the chaps name was Hugh Russell; he had served in the army, was well made, and may live in Knight St. Bury.

I could not thank Karen enough—the name was right, Hugh had been in the army, (I had received a letter from Hugh while I was with my Foster parents in Liverpool, and he had been in the army-in Germany) Unfortunately we moved shortly

afterwards, and the letter went missing. I had always kept the letter in a little red handbag, which I had been given as a present. During the move the bag was misplaced. Hugh assumed he had had the wrong address, and I did not have his address. And so we lost contact again.

Following Karen's phone call, (a few days later), we went up to Bury with a bunch of flowers for the reporter who had helped me so much to get this search started.

We mentioned about Hugh to her. She went into the office, and a few minutes later, she came back and said that Hugh did live in Knight St. and also gave us his house number, telephone number, and a map showing how to get to Hugh's home.

We could not believe our luck!!

As it was getting late, we thought that we would go home and phone Hugh first thing in the morning.

I hardly slept.

What would he be like?

Would he accept me after all these years apart, or would he not want to know me?

What was his health like; because whichever way I made contact it was going to be a shock to him?

Living in Hope

Over breakfast the next morning, Tom and I discussed the best way to make contact, and decided to phone him first. Tom would phone him, and if everything was all right, and Hugh was willing, Tom would pass the phone to me.

Tom phoned Hugh, and said that although they had never met, they could be related to each other. Hugh was interested, and asked Tom to carry on. So Tom asked him if he had a sister called Margaret. I certainly do –he said, but I have no idea where she is, it is over fifty years since we last saw each other. She is a year younger than me.

That was it:-

I HAD FOUND MY ELDEST BROTHER

Tom told Hugh, that he was my husband and that I was standing alongside the phone. He immediately told Tom to put me on the phone. That was all I needed.

HUGH HAD ACCEPTED ME.

I took the phone off Tom, and as soon as I spoke, Hugh said that in all the years we had been apart, he had never forgotten that my birthday was November 10, but he had never had an address to send a card to. We made arrangements to go up to Bury to meet Hugh at his home, the following afternoon

Tom and I started off after lunch, it took us just over an hour, We did not know what to expect- a chap of 60-

living on his own- but as we both said, it doesn't matter he is my family. We arrived at Hugh's, the door was open, and I knocked on the door. Hugh said to come in, and there we stood, face-to-face together after fifty-six years. He was a bit on the quiet side, probably wondering what we wanted, after all these years, but when we said that we had been trying for years, and with him moving around so much, we had not had any luck until the Bury Times feature, and Karen's phone call.

While we were talking, I had a good look at Hugh; he was so smart with well-polished brown brogue shoes-I felt so proud of him. His flat was spotless probably due to his time in the army.

Hugh told Tom and I that he had been in the army for National Service at 18 years old, and had come out, but could not settle down, so he had re-enlisted in the Royal Lancashire Fusiliers, and served in Germany and Cyprus.

When he left the army, he travelled around quite a lot to various jobs, he even worked on repairing roads in Liverpool we were so close yet so far apart. He was then forced to retire with arthritis.

During the last eight years, Hugh had become diabetic, and had to inject himself twice a day. He also had cataracts, and was partially blind, for which he attended hospital, his next appointment was the following week.

He had to phone up a couple of days before to book a sitting ambulance, to take him to the hospital.

Living in Hope

I asked Hugh if he would like us to take him to the hospital, in the car, instead of by ambulance—a big grin spread over his face—he said yes, then thought—but you will have to travel from Liverpool. We assured him that it was no problem. The following week we went up to Hugh's early, in plenty of time for the hospital—he was ready, and had a `brew` ready when we arrived. The problem with Hugh's eyes was probably as a result of his Diabetes

We continued to take Hugh to every appointment, and visited in between, we had a lot of catching up to do.

During our visits, Hugh talked about his past life, before we had met again: -He often mentioned Jericho –the workhouse to where we were all taken when we were `split up`. The building still stands in the Fairfield Hospital, and is now an office block near the main entrance,

He said that he hated Jericho, and within a few days of arriving, had run away, but the police had found him at Buckhurst—near the duck pond, and cottage from where we were taken.

He was taken to a home in Lancaster, and when he arrived he found out that our brother James was already there. He would not go into any more detail, except to say they were treated very badly.

We found, as we got to know Hugh better, that he would not go into detail and as a result we accepted it (obviously). He would go quiet, (deep in thought), and sometimes there were a few tears. I can understand this, because I feel the same emotion with my past, when I think of certain times, when I felt so very, very hurt, and alone.

Hugh told us that he had found our Mum, before she died in 1981 aged 67 years, and that her health was not too good. He stayed with her, for a time, to try and help her. She had gangrene in her foot, and was also diabetic. The gangrene spread into Mum's leg, and she had to have her leg amputated, she never left hospital. Hugh got very upset at this stage, and stopped talking.

Hugh has had a very sad life –with nobody to help him through—but I am here for him now and I will never let him down.

Some six months later, we were still visiting Hugh a few times each week.

Pat, his friend from next door, phoned me to say that Hugh was not too well, but she would keep an eye on him. Early the next morning, I phoned Pat and she said that Hugh was no better, So I asked her to phone Hugh's doctor. Later, she phoned me to say that Hugh had refused to see the doctor, because he had his two cats to think about—Fluffy and Tinkerbell, and she thought he was getting worse. So I asked Pat to phone the doctor, no matter what Hugh said, and I asked her to put Hugh on the phone.

I asked him, who would look after the cats, if anything happened to him, If he had to go into hospital, I would look after them with Pat. He then agreed to see the

Living in Hope

doctor, who said he should be in hospital, and arranged an ambulance.

By this time, I had been able to contact Tom, and we were on our way up to Bury—while we where travelling, the ambulance had arrived, and Hugh was on his way to hospital.

During the journey his condition had became worse, his sugar level was very high, and he was admitted to A and E. While in A and E he was asked for his next of kin, and he told them –"my sister Margaret."

It was only a short while later that he went Hypo, due to his high level of sugar

We arrived at the hospital, while Hugh was Hypo, and immediately spoke to the doctor, who was with Hugh. The doctor asked if I was Margaret, Hugh's sister and I said that I was. He explained, that Hugh had told them that I was his next of kin, but did not know our address—only our phone number, which he had at home. He gave him all the information he needed about me. Then he asked me if I knew what medication Hugh was taking-I did not, and suddenly I began to realize how little I knew about Hugh's medical condition. Before now we had always been talking about the past, not the present..

Tom and I went to Hugh's home to find his medication—it only took about ten minutes. We found his insulin in the fridge, some of which was out of date, and it appeared that he had not been taking the right amount. He had plenty of cat food in, as expected, so with his insulin, toiletries, and nightwear, we went back to the hospital. On the way, Tom and I both realized that Hugh's eyes were worse than we had thought—and that would account for the problems with the insulin.

When we arrived at the hospital, we handed the medication to the staff on the ward, who immediately gave it to the doctor.

I thought that once they got his sugar level down, it would not be long before he would be home. But no. Hugh suffered a stroke, affecting his speech and throat, and all down his left side

We went up from Liverpool every day to see him, while he was in hospital.

On one of the visits, our daughter Sue said she would like to come with us, to meet her uncle Hugh for the first time. This made me happy, as Sue will not travel far since a car crash two years ago. It was also her birthday.

We all went to Hugh's ward, he was wrapped up in blankets, the nurse said that he had lost his body heat, and the doctor would like a word with us.

The doctor came to the bedside, and asked if he could have a word in the day room, which was empty, so we followed him to the day room. He told us that the next few hours were crucial, He apologized for having to ask the question, but said that if Hugh had a heart attack, or possibly another stroke, do they have my permission not to resuscitate, as his quality of life would be nil, and the permission could only be given by the next of kin. I explained, that I had to talk to my other brothers' and sister, about it, but I would accept the responsibility, and gave my permission. We felt so sorry for our Sue, as it was the first time she had seen her uncle Hugh, and her mum had had to discuss resuscitation.

When we came back to Liverpool, I phoned the rest of the family, and explained the situation to them, they all agreed that I had made the right decision. The following day, we went back up to the hospital, the doctor said there was a slight improvement in Hugh's general condition. James, my brother, had phoned me, and I agreed to meet him and his wife Sandra at the hospital the next day. James had quite a shock when he saw his brother, even though we had prepared him.

James had spent a lot of time with Hugh in his early days. From then on James went to the hospital, during the day, getting the bus into Bury, from Yorkshire, and Tom and I in the evenings, after Tom had finished work- - at the weekend we would pick them up.

Gaynor, our eldest daughter, came up to the hospital to see Hugh, as often as her nursing duties allow.

Hugh remained in hospital for the next seven weeks, and shocked every body, he pulled through, and he is a real fighter, even though he is restricted to moving around in a wheel chair.

As Hugh was getting stronger, I told him he owed me 56 birthday cards, but if he sang ` happy birthday` to me I would let him off, he surprised us all ,and in a lovely voice he sang it to me.Hugh was on the way back, even though his voice was slurred we could understand him.

Gaynor our eldest daughter, took me up to see Hugh, as often as she could as Tom has had to go back to work. James, my brother, and Sandra his wife, have been a tower of strength to us. Gemma, Sue's daughter and Aimee Gaynor, s daughter (our two granddaughters), loved to visit their uncle Hugh. and take him his favourite toffee,(Diabetic). This he loved and talked to them for long periods about school and what they had been doing since he had last seen them.

During a visit when Tom, James, and I were at the hospital, the Sister asked us to a meeting, a few days later, to discuss Hugh's discharge. Present at the meeting was the Sister, Physiotherapist, and Alistair, Hugh's social worker, in the hospital. We had met Alistair the day after Hugh had been admitted to hospital, and he had kept in constant touch with us right through out Hugh's stay, he helped us a tremendous amount to get through the social service systems.

The physiotherapist said there was nothing they could do, as Hugh would not, co-operate. The Sister said that Hugh's medication was now sorted out. There was no need for him to stay in hospital. We were told that Hugh could not go back to his own home, because he would need twenty four hour care, and suggested we look for a nursing home for him.

Alistair gave us some brochures, and said he would help in any way he could. Hugh had always said that he wanted to go back to Ramsbottom.

Living in Hope

Looking through the brochures, we saw one in Ramsbottom, called the Cliff.Alistair phoned me at home, and said he could recommend a good one in Ramsbottom. It was the same one that we had seen in the brochures.

That evening, after visiting Tom and I went to the Cliff, to see what it was like. We were shown a few different rooms, and in particular, one large room with a big bay window, over looking a lovely garden and the moors, where we had once lived.

When we got home, I went on the phone, and phoned James and Sandra, our brother John, (who, due to having diabetes, could not, do as much) and our sister Alice, who lives in Nottingham.

We arranged to meet in Ramsbottom, the following Sunday, and go to see the home to-gether. We all decided that it would be all right for Hugh, and asked the Sister if we could take it for Hugh. There was no problem.

Hugh would not consider going into a nursing home. So we decided to tell him it was a small hospital in Ramsbottom, we told him about the room we had found for him, and he would be moving soon.

Mean time James, Tom, and I, sorted out Hugh's home, A few trips in the car, saw his TV and stereo, and other items moved into his new home. Gaynor husband later took his three piece suite. We held back on the suite because we had not been able to find a home for Hugh's cats, and at this stage James and Sandra said that they would take them to their home. Pat, Hugh's neighbour had looked after the cats the whole time Hugh was in hospital. But could not have them permanently

On the fourth of September 2002 Hugh was settled into his new home, I asked Hugh if he liked it. He said it would do for the time being, until he was able to go home. I would sit by the side of his chair, and the next thing he would say was "I would love some toffee", I would put a piece in his mouth, and then a big grin would spread across his face, then the twinkle appeared in his eye. His whole face lit up, he looked so happy when we were there, we hated leaving him.

I often thought about bringing Hugh back to Liverpool, to be nearer to us, but I did not think he would stand the journey and it would also have doubled James's journey from Yorkshire. It was a lot easier for Tom and I to travel to Bury by car.

While Hugh was in hospital, we had had to cancel his appointments at Birch Hill hospital in Rochdale for his eyes, and now had to pick them up again.

Hugh asked me to go with him to the hospital for his appointments. At times, we were leaving home at 6.30 in the morning. I went in the ambulance, and Tom carried on in the car to meet James, and then meet Hugh and I at the hospital On our way in the ambulance, Hugh and I would pass Owd Betts (a pub on the moor,) not far from the cottage where we had lived all those years ago. I told Hugh where we were, and he got very upset. I put my arms around him, and he said we must never leave one

Living in Hope

another again. We held hands all the way to the hospital, and promised we would never part again.

Hugh asked us to take him around Ramsbottom, and we promised that one day we would. He wanted to see his old haunts. The problem was that Hugh could not stand while we transferred him from the wheelchair into the car.

When I came home, I phoned mobility in Blackpool, and asked about a car, explaining Hugh's situation to them, but they told me there was a twelve month waiting list, but they would see what they could do to help us, I told Hugh that I had put in for a car, so that we could take him out He said he wanted a picnic on the moors. We went along with him to keep up his moral.

On one occasion when we visited Hugh he said his foot was sore, and complained all night, so I went to see the sister in charge, apparently she had put a dressing on and had called the doctor, as Hugh had a pressure sore on his ankle.

Hugh said his leg was hurting and he did not seem to be too good. The bandage on his heel had come loose, so having worked in nursing homes before, I decided to take a look at his heel, and saw the pressure sore, which was quite nasty, I went to see the Sister, who had not realized we where visiting, and she told me that the doctor had been in, and seen Hugh, and prescribed antibiotics.

It was shortly after this, that we began to feel that Hugh was starting to give up. When we went to see him he cried a lot , and pleaded with us not to let him go to Jericho, he had obviously been thinking of our mum.

He wanted to go and see our Grandparents and Auntie Alice ,but we had to remind him that they were no longer with us.

Hugh got very upset and we tried to change the subject but he kept coming back to the same subject again. This went on for a few more visits ,

On another visit a nurse was trying to give him a drink. All of his drinks had to thickened, because water was making him choke.

Looking at him, I wondered if he had had a small stroke, as we were discussing this among our selves ,Silvia the sister came into Hugh's room, and said she was waiting for the doctor to come, as she felt that he now had renal failure, and was measuring his fluid intake and output. Sylvia has been brilliant through out, both looking after Hugh, and also helping us ,the family.

I had a phone call from the mobility people, to say they had a car for Hugh, and could they go to the home to demonstrate it to Hugh. I said I would phone the home, and ask the sister, but she said that Hugh was not well enough,

Shortly after this, Sylvia phoned us at home, to say that Hugh had to go back into hospital-the doctor had been, and he also thought that Hugh had renal failure.

I managed to get hold of Tom, and we went straight up to the home, in Ramsbottom, As we pulled into the drive, an ambulance was coming out. We were not

Living in Hope

sure who was in the ambulance. The sister said we had just missed Hugh, as he had just left for hospital. We immediately went to the hospital. When we arrived, Hugh was unconscious, and his temperature was sky high. We stayed with him while he was taken to an admission ward, and the staff said his condition was stable.

I had phoned my brother James and told him the situation about Hugh, I stayed with Hugh, while Tom went to pick up James and Sandra from Todmorden in Yorkshire., When they came into the ward we could see from James's face how upset they were, We stayed for a while, the doctor said the situation had not changed, and that the no resuscitation still stood

As there was no immediate change expected, we all decided to go home, as it was four o'clock in the morning.

Next day, I phoned the mobility and told them that Hugh had been taken into hospital, and they said that they would hold the car until Hugh came out of hospital and would we keep them informed.

As Tom was working, our Gaynor took me up to see Hugh, he had regained consciousness, but he was still on oxygen. We just talked to him about what we would do, when he got better.

Hugh was moved to another ward, and he seemed, to be improving, He was trying to talk, and to our amazement, said he was hungry. He also said he wanted a whisky. Gaynor and I told the doctor as she was on her rounds. She said that she would see to it. This was

THURSDAY and the doctor said that we would have another meeting to discuss Hugh's general condition in the middle of next week.

The very next day FRIDAY, all the family were there, including James daughter Joanne. When Tom and I walked in Alistair (Social Worker) came and sat by me, and said they were moving Hugh to a side ward. We thought that this was because Hugh had been making a noise during the night, and had been disturbing the rest of the patients, and this would allow them to get some sleep. Imagine how we felt, when Alistair told us that Hugh was starting his pathway to heaven. We asked what the pathway was, as we had never heard this saying before. We were then told that Hugh did not have long to live, I could not believe it. Only the day before the doctor had told us that we would have a meeting the following week about Hugh's condition, and the same day he had been asking for food and drink.

I couldn't take it in, I broke down in tears, Hugh and I had promised never to leave each other again, but now that promise was coming to an end.

How can this be happening?

I love Hugh so much.

What am I going to do now?

On the Saturday, it was our brother John's son's wedding, which the whole family went to. We stayed for a short while after the ceremony, but my mind was at the hospital, Tom, James, Sandra , and I went to the hospital, when we arrived sister Alice and Bill were already there

Living in Hope

,Alice had not been able to visit much as she lived in Nottingham,

Not long after we arrived, Alice and Bill had to leave, as they had a long journey ahead of them,. After they had gone James ,Sandra ,and Tom ,went for a smoke I stayed with Hugh, I was wiping his face, when he tried to say something to me, I feel so guilty, because I couldn't make out what it was. Was he asking for a drink? I will never know, he just looked at me.,

Just then the door opened and our Gaynor and Aimee came to see their Uncle Hugh. They had driven all the way from Liverpool on their own to give us their support.

Hugh always called Aimee (his little Aimee). Although she was only seven, she had drawn a picture of her Uncle Hugh and stuck it on the window, so he could look at it.

As it was getting towards nine o-clock, we had to make a decision whether to stay or not, if the worst happened I wanted to be there. So after a talk to the staff and the family, we were told that Hugh could last a few more days, and it was decided that we would come home

Joanne took James and Sandra home, Gaynor and Aimee followed us in their car, but all the way home I felt that I should have stayed with Hugh.

I had a strange feeling that something was going to happen.

That night, I had a dream that Hugh and I were back in Ramsbottom, we were walking over the bridge of the river Irwell, we were ten years of age, the age when we left Ramsbottom. I was in a summer dress and Hugh had a grey jumper and grey trousers ,we were walking up Peel Brow then onto the lanes that would lead us up to Buckhurst.Walking up the lane, by the chapel, I had just said to Hugh how hot the sun was and the light so bright. We arrived at the little chapel by the duck pond,. I turned to look at Hugh he just smiled and waved to me. I woke suddenly when the phone rang I knew it was the hospital to tell me that Hugh had just died- the time was 4:56 so Hugh was not alone ,I was there in spirit back at the place where we were so happy.

God bless Hugh until we meet again

We went to pick up Sandra and James, and went along to the hospital to say our goodbye.

We arranged for Hugh's funeral to take place at St, Paul's Church in Ramsbottom on third of June2003. He had the Union Jack draped over his coffin, with his beret and hackle from the Royal Lancashire Fusiliers. He was so proud to have served with them.His coffin was saluted as he passed into church, by the Royal British Legion, I think we gave Hugh the send off that he would have liked. Hugh is now resting with all the people he spoke about, his beloved Grandparents, Aunt Alice, and our mum.

I will never forget Hugh saying that he now had a family that cared, including his two nieces, Gemma and his little Aimee

I have to say before I finish that we now have a beautiful great granddaughter (Hollie) we send our congratulations to Gemma our Granddaughter for such a precious gift.

Part 4
Alice's story

CHAPTER 1
RAMSBOTTOM

Alice aged 5

I can remember living in a big house in Ramsbottom, which I have now found out, was Fir Street in Ramsbottom. It was where our Mum, Dad, Grandma and Grandpa, my eldest brother Hughie, my sister Margaret, Jimmy, and John, my two younger brothers lived. It was Grandma and Grandpas house.

I can remember that we were all very happy living in our Grandparents house. They had a very big garden in which we all played, and across the road in front of the house I played with other children and my sister Margaret, making tea and cakes with stones and slates for cups and saucers, and other items we found on the building site.

We all played very well together and enjoyed each others company.

But then a terrible thing happened. Our Grandma died, and at that time I was too young to under stand why I could not see her again.

In those days, people who died were kept in the front room of the house, where people could pay their last respects to the person who had died.

One day, I climbed on a chair near Grandma, and climbed in the coffin with her, and went to sleep, as I used to before she died

The people in the house were all looking for me; the last place they looked was in the coffin, not the place you would expect to find me.

You see ,Grandma always sat in a big armchair, at one side of the big coal fire ,with me on her knee, while Grandpa, sat on the other side with Margaret on his knee.

I remember them being very loving people, I could not understand why I could not speak to her again.

I felt so lonely without her, but my sister Margaret was always there to make me smile again.

Shortly after what must have been the funeral, we slept in one bed. We looked at the bottom of the bed and saw a lady in white, and a light behind her head. I was told it was Grandma, who had come to say good-by to us. I remember all the children being frightened and Hughie telling us not to cry.

Living in Hope

I believe when I started school my Dad took me, I do not remember this, but my school records show this.

The next thing I remember, was that we all went to stay with Auntie Alice, and our cousins Fred and Jean, at 5 Mount Street, There was a big square of grass in front of Mount Street, with houses all around, and in one of the houses lived an old man who used to tell me stories,

On bonfire night we would all gather round a big fire, which had a guy on top that our brother Hughie had made, the people were always very friendly, as I remember.

Margaret and I would go to the woods, and collect daisies to put round our necks. If we ran out of flowers our brother Jimmy would go and collect more for us.

The things I remember about Mount Street was a door that went under the stairs, our Hughie and Fred would say in fun that if we were naughty they would put us under there with the rats, but of course there were no rats to be seen, it made us behave our selves, To this day I do not like rats.

I remember in Auntie Alice's front room there was an organ, and a man who played it, later I found out it was my Dad. He was a tall man with dark hair. He would let me sit by him while he played the organ. Above the organ was a picture of a man with a white beard, all fluffy and he was so smart, in a dark suit and a white shirt. I loved that picture, and it always stayed in my mind.

One day, Auntie Alice had gone to the corner shop, and left us playing in the kitchen, where there was a big table, around which we all had our meals. My brother Jimmy and I started playing cowboys and Indians around the table. He shouted my name and I looked up. The poker came flying at me and hit me like an arrow on the front of my head. It started to bleed, and I had to go to hospital, because I needed stitches in my forehead.

Auntie Alice was very cross with Jimmy, but it taught me a lesson, never to look up when some one shouts my name.

Some time later, I caught Scarlet Fever and was admitted to hospital.In those days Scarlet fever was very serious, and I was admitted to an Isolation ward. I can remember the ambulance men carrying me from Auntie Alice's house, passed the old man, who was so concerned; he was asking what was wrong with me. The ambulance men told him. I had been wrapped up in a large red blanket which I asked if I could keep it, but I was told they needed for other children.

I was missing my Mum. I was put in a room on my own, which had a big glass window. When I did see Mum and Auntie Alice it was only through the glass window.

The next thing I remember was when we left Auntie Alice's house, and went to live on the moors, in a cottage, above Ramsbottom. It was an old building but it seemed to be the next best place to Grandmas and Auntie Alice's.

We were very poor. We all slept in one room, the cooking was all done on the fire as there was no gas or electricity. The water had to be collected from a stream

Living in Hope

nearby. But it was home, for all of us to be together. It was every thing we had in the world, but we were so happy there.

My sister Margaret, started at the chapel school, I was too young. I wanted to go every where with Margaret, and I cried because I could not go to school with her. One day, I was told that I could go to school, if I sat quiet, and did some drawing, which I did.

I held her hand and walked all the way to school and back, holding my head up high, as I was with my big sister. It made me feel so good inside. I was so proud of Margaret, and I was a big girl coming home from school.

Margaret can remember the water fall at the side of our cottage but I cannot remember it, there are parts that I cannot remember, as I have blank spots.

I can remember the stream, where I used to play with my brother Jimmy, throwing stones in the water, and getting twigs and leaves, to make boats and letting them float down stream, to see which one got there first. It was great fun.

There was only one cottage next to ours, where an old man with ducks lived. I liked the old man and his ducks. He let me collect the duck eggs for him every day, and always let me have the first one. He sat out side the cottage, on an old chair. He used to talk to me and he was just like Grandpa to me.. I don't know what happened to the old man, but the cottages and the old man were very happy times, with Mum and Dad, and the family, which were to stay with me for the rest of my life.

I can remember one day, when Margaret had to look after all of us, as Mum had to go into hospital, for a short stay. She came home with a lovely surprise, a little brother called Stephen, he was so small. Mum made us all sit down so we could hold the baby. He was so lovely, and now there were six of us.

Mum could not afford a new cot, so Stephen had to sleep in the bottom drawer of the side board.

I can remember Stephen was bathed in an old sink, in the kitchen, with water which was brought from the stream, and heated on the fire.

I can also remember that when it was winter I had no coat, just a cardigan and summer dress.

We went across the fields to the market, and on the way, we would stop at a farm, where the farmers wife would have some home made cakes. We sat by a big open fire, which was very warm. She made her own bread and when we called on the way home, she would give us a loaf.

By the time we got to the market, it was closing time, so we picked up fruit and vegetables from under the stalls to take home. This had to last us until the next week.

It must have been very hard times for our Mum and Dad to make ends meet but we were the happiest family in the world. There was no help in those days.

The worst happened again. The old man from next door came and told us to hide in the bushes at the back

Living in Hope

of the house, and wait until he called us again. Margaret was at school.

I heard what seemed to me was soldiers, coming over the bridge. I can still hear the sound of their boots on the stone road way. I will never forget it. It must have been the police, coming to take Mum and Dad away, and the children were also taken from our beloved cottage on the moor.

It was a very sad day for our parents and family. People do not know what happens to families when things like this happen, unless it happens to them. I did not see Margaret again she was taken out of school

CHAPTER 2
JERICHO

When I arrived at Jericho which was on the outskirts of Bury Margaret was there but we did not know where our brothers had gone to

Later James and Hughie joined us before they went to the men's side of the workhouse we went to the ladies side.

I can remember the boys playing on what I thought was a garden roller, it started to move, and I started towards the boys ,I shouted for them to jump off, which they did, and the roller ran down a steep runway and crashed into some doors, they were all covered in like a conservatory.

Hughie ran away, as he did not like the place, Margaret and I were taken into this long room with beds all down one side, with older ladies in them, and then we were told to go to bed.

I wanted to go to the toilet, so Margaret started walking me down this long room, at the bottom of the room was the toilet , which was open for every one to see a lady in a long white nightdress, put her arms out in front of her, and started walking towards us she must have been sleep walking, I had never seen any thing like it before It frightened me ,I thought it must be a ghost

Living in Hope

I fell into the toilet, my feet in the air, was all that could be seen of me.

First Margaret, then I, were taken to a children's orphanage. It was a big place with lots of boys and girls

While I was there, I was taken ill, and put in the sick ward. I met a girl there and I was given some tablets to take, I could not swallow them, so she told me to put the tablets under the mattress, which I did, and got caught, I was smacked very hard by the nurse. I did not like that ward, and I had not got Margaret with me, I missed her so very much.

When we were at the home we had to walk behind one another in twos to go to church,

I heard one little girl say to her Mummy, look that little girl is wearing my dress we sent to the jumble sale. I felt so hurt and cheap, because we had every ones cast off clothes.

When it was Easter, we sat round the breakfast table, the Saturday before Easter Sunday. All the children, had a hard boiled egg out of the bowl, and sat down, and painted a pattern on it. We then got it back on Easter morning for breakfast. We also had a ration of sweets, dolly mixtures I remember, each weekend, I found out later from Margaret that she handed her sweets over to the big boys, as they would hit me if she did not.

Margaret and I did not like it there very much, we got in with a girl called Jean. She said that we could break out.

One day she told us to hide in the bushes, when no one was looking, we ran off, we walked for ages, and I was getting tired. We saw two ladies coming towards us, and Margaret asked them did they know where our Mum lived. They said they would find her for us, and gave us some ice-cream One lady went into another room, and phoned the police, as they had heard on the radio that three girls had run away from a home, back to the home we went.

The next thing that I knew, we were in a big cold building with wooden seats, a horrible cold place, we were then taken into another big room where we were questioned. Margaret was brought into the room, and I was frightened and crying, Margaret came over and held my hand with James, this made us feel a bit better, but I knew Margaret was upset, I was later told by Margaret that we had been in a court room

From that day I never saw our Mum and Dad again, for many years.

CHAPTER 3
QUEENSFERRY

Shortly after that, we were taken to Foster parents in North Wales. They lived in a lovely bungalow, and we were fostered there for a short time Mr H bought me my first pot headed and rag bodied doll. It was the first doll I had ever had in my life (well any thing of my own in the toy line).

I loved that doll and loved Mr H for buying it for me.

I can remember Mr H taking Margaret, and I for new clothes, to a big shop. We had dresses, coats, cardigans, under wear socks and shoes bought for us. It was great

Mrs H worked at the picture house as Manageress. We often went with her, and looked round the seats to see if anyone had left any thing behind by mistake.

There was a long lane, where we played at the back of the bungalow, and one day Margaret who had a bike really hurt herself, and damaged the bike. Mrs H was very cross with her.

One more time Mrs H was cross with Margaret when she left Margaret to give me a bath. I fell in the bath and hurt my back. I was crying when she came home from work. Mrs H went mad again as she should never have left us alone and never left Margaret to bath me. She could have got into terrible trouble. I remember she threw Margaret down the hall way and Margaret really cried.

It was not long after that, that Margaret left. I was asked if I wanted to go with her. I was too young at that time and did not know what was going on; I said I wanted to stay. That night I went to bed on my own and cried for Margaret. I had never been with out her before, Mrs H never came in to see if I was alright and the next day I was on my way to my next home.

CHAPTER 4
LIVERPOOL

My next home was to a Mr and Mrs Grundy, at 6 Woodbine St, Kirk dale, with Auntie Sarah, Mrs Grundy's sister. I was seven years old now I had not been to school much, as I do not remember it. I was sent to Daisy Street School, just across the road. I liked it at this school, but one day, the teacher gave me the cane for talking in Prayers, I did not do it again.

While I was living with Mrs Grundy I suffered a lot of throat problems, till I got a bit older, but she always looked after me. I settled in with Mr Mrs Grundy very well, it seemed I had landed on my feet at last, I was happy; I started talking about my own Mum and Dad in Ramsbottom and my brothers and sister.

One day I had a visitor it was my sister Margaret, it made me so happy. My sister and her foster sister Lilian did my hair for me it looked lovely.

I was about seven years old by this time. But it happened again I was getting to close to my sister, my Mum got jealous and stopped me seeing her, and I was so upset.

Finally I settled down again, my mum found out my feet were bad so she bought me a pair of Clarke's sandals called (start right heels), it soon put my feet right. See, she really cared about me.

She also sent me to Ballet and tap dancing school. I entered lot of exams, and passed most of them, bronze, silver, and gold, plus lots of certificates.

The dancing teacher was called Miss Barbra Wolfe. She was a very good teacher and was well known in Liverpool in the 1950s and 60s.

We danced at the American air base camp at Burtonwood, Warrington, it was great. I also did national dance as I got older.

I later joined the Methodist Church, and went to Sunday school classes, and all kinds of church activities, singing in many concerts I had a very full life.

I used to love it when my foster Mum met me from school on a Friday. We would go shopping down Scotland road, and to the market. Mum would buy me sweets, which I would chose for my self I kept them in a small jar that was on the sideboard, and they would have to last me all week.

I also had lots of friends, like Iris and Pamela, but my best friend was Iris.

Every Sunday morning, I had to go to church with my Mum. I did not mind going with my Mum but three times a day was a bit much It was a day when we put our best clothes on and got dressed up. It was different from being in the home, wearing second hand clothes, and people's cast offs.

At Easter we got a lot of Easter Eggs, I had a lot of Aunties and Uncles as mum and Dad came from big families, Christmas and Birthdays were the same.

Living in Hope

I can remember I got a present and card from my real Mum and Auntie Alice, they were lovely, a shiny card with my age on it and flowers in the numbers. I will always remember them.

As I got older, I started going out with my friend Shirley. We went every where together. She was more like a sister, and made me think of my sister Margaret I was not allowed see even though we were only a couple of miles a part

We went to night school for short hand typing. We also went to Lambeth road school in the evening for Art classes.

We often went to the Cavern in Liverpool, as Shirley worked in an office in town.

My summer holidays where spent in Colwyn Bay, with my Auntie Mowner, and my cousins Ruth and David, I went from school, once a week to Bedford Road, to see Auntie Poll. I really enjoyed Sunday nights after church when we went to Auntie Essies and Uncle Bobs, in Wadham Road, Bootle Auntie Nelly would be there. We would go for supper and I got to stay up late. They had a big family with twin boys Brian and Alan, Leslie, Bob and Ronnie. They had a big table, full of all sorts of food, it was great, the twins and I were about the same age, so we got on really well. We were very happy, as we watched the Generation game with Bruce Forsythe, it was great because we got to stay up late. The rest of the week I had to go to bed early for school.

When I was eleven I would go to Bootle Grammar school to play tennis. The Beatles were often there, before they became famous. I liked Ringo the best.

At Woodbine Street, we did not have a bathroom, in those days we had a tin bath, which was kept in the back yard, hanging on a big nail on the wall. On bath night the bath was brought in and filled with hot water, the water was heated on the stove, with big pans and Mum put Dettol in to make it smell nice, it was lovely. After we had all had our baths the water was used to swill the yard, so it was kept clean, we had some fun tipping the water out, some one always got there feet wet. The wall was painted with a mixture of lime and Dolly Blue with cold water.

Across the road in my school, down in the cellar we had Irish Reel dancing twice a week, it was good and I liked it very much.

In the next street, Harkel, lived a lady called Mrs Davies who I called Auntie Annie, she was Mums best friend and neighbour. In her back yard was an air raid shelter, which had been used during the war, when the docks in Bootle and Liverpool had been badly bombed. Mum told me one night she heard the sirens warning of another air raid, and they would have to run into the shelter, If Mum had stayed in the house she would have been killed as a bomb blew the back door and windows out.

My Mum still had food coupons and as a little girl I would play Post Office and shops with my best friend Iris.

Living in Hope

and I met Mum there, and we would walk home together. I used to baby sit for Auntie Polls daughter Joan, looking after Irene and Robert and I was taken home on his Motor bike and side car I loved that bike.

I joined a Methodist Youth club. My uncle Bob used to help run it, we would go hiking with other youth clubs to Derbyshire and we also went swimming.

My friend Shirley and I went on a meat traders outing. It was a trip on the River Mersey on a boat called the Royal Iris which was known as " the fish and chip boat". The boat went up the Mersey almost to Southport and there was a raffle for which we sold tickets for half the night, while the dance was going on.

That is where I met Mike Wade, he was to play a big part in my life. I started dating him, he lived in Nottingham, but he was working at the Royal Liverpool Telephone exchange, and his digs were in Bootle, in the same road as the Beatles,

We went dancing and to the pictures, and eating out in Restaraunts. We went to Birkenhead and Wales, at the weekends, we also went to the beach for walks, little did I know that my Sister Margaret lived by the Five Lamps, I would have loved to have seen her again.

Some times we would go to Blackpool on the fair ground we went with Alex and his wife Barbara at that time , I did not realize what a big part in our lives they would play, because I was17 years old when I got engaged to Mike, when I reached 19 ,we decided to get married.

So we started to save for a house which we bought in Long Eaton, Nottingham

CHAPTER 5
NOTTINGHAM

We were married at a register office in Liverpool on the 3rd March 1960 then we had four good years together we had two dogs, Timmy and Bob, we took them walking in the Derbyshire Dales.

I had a good job working in an office at Ericsons in the 60s

We went climbing round Snowdon in Wales and nearly lost our dog Bob when he got the scent of the sheep and Mike had to go looking for him. The shepherd said that if Bob put a foot wrong he could fall down a crevice and would not be able to get out any way we did find him with the shepherds help thank goodness

When I became pregnant with Shaun, Bob started showing his teeth and not getting off the chair when I told him to. I had to get Mike from work as Bob nearly bit me. We took him to the vet, he said there was nothing wrong with him but then Bob showed his teeth again, the vet asked was I pregnant, I did not know at this time but the dog new, the vet suggested that we find a new home for him as he could attack the Baby when it was born. So we found a lovely couple that lived in Castle Donnington, they were a lovely old couple and they really took to Bob

When we started with the Baby we had a power cut so we would listen to the battery radio, it was an Irish play, and in it the babies name was Shaun, we both decided to call our baby Shaun when it was born, and Audrey if it was a girl.

We were to have a son Shaun; it was the happiest day of my life when he was born, in a nursing home called the Grove Shardlow. When I was carrying Shaun I nearly lost him, but when he was born he had very dark hair and blue eyes, He was the best thing in my life and well worth the wait.

Mike was over the moon when he saw he had a son, and so was his Dad. We had kept the name Wade going. His Granddad was Irish and pleased that I had given him a Grandson. He bought me a necklace of Green white stones, Shamrock, it was lovely. There was a bond between Shaun and Granddad that was to last forever.

While I was waiting to have Shaun, I made lots of clothes for him and bought a silver Cross pram.

I loved being at home with Shaun doing the things that all new Mums do, I loved taking Shaun out in his pram to the park feeding him and most of all loving him.

When Shaun was 14 months old a bombshell hit us. We had been on holiday to Skegness, and on the way home Shaun took ill, with a temperature, the next day , which was Sunday, he was crying a lot, so on the Monday we decided to get the Doctor but after I put him to bed I listened at the bottom of the stairs, I don't know why, I

Living in Hope

suppose it was a mothers instinct, I heard funny noises, I ran up the stairs , and got the shock of my life, I couldn't see Shaun for the bubbles all over his head, I shouted for Mike to come, he came up and said ; My God; and ran to Shaun as he was blue in the face, Mike said to phone the Doctor, in the meantime Mike had taken Shaun to the bathroom, and was trying to get Shaun to breath.

We decided the Doctor was taking too long, so we rushed down to the fire station were we knew they would have Oxygen. The firemen fought long and hard to save Shaun, When the doctor arrived thank goodness it was our own doctor.

Doctor Morley gave Shaun an injection in the throat, and rushed him to Chestnut Grove Children's hospital, It was thanks to all the firemen in all the hard work and the Ambulance men, who said all you can do now is pray as every moment counts, I have never prayed so hard in all my life, and I thank God that we made it in time

Shaun was in hospital for two weeks, with pneumonia and Epilepsy, he was only 14 months old, he was a bright baby, walking and talking at seven months, he lost that, and had to learn all over again, he had good will power. The Doctors said he was fighting all the way.

I never prayed so hard for God to save my beloved son, my little baby boy.

It was a very stressful time, and I thought it was all over when he came out of hospital, little did we know that it was just the beginning, and was to stay with him for the rest of his life.

He was in and out of hospital for weeks at a time; I spent most of my time at his bed side,

I hated coming home at night, in case any thing happened to him, and I was not there, Mike was with me, when he was not working, you could not stay over night with the children like you can to day.

I lived a life not knowing whether I was coming or going.

When Shaun was about three years old, my Doctor suggested I put Shaun in a day nursery and take a part time job so that we could have a break from one another, as I was heading for a break down ,I had previously finished work at Erickson's as there was no maternity leave in those days,

We got a day nursery place at Plessey and they gave me a job, but it was full time.

It helped Shaun mix with other children and gave me time to my self.

It seemed to work out well for all of us even thought it was hard work, Mike and I were able to have our meals together and most of all talk to one another.

Shaun started school at the infants, but he was not there long, as I was told that he would have to go to a special school, Fox Wood at Eastwood, the Teachers at a normal school were not allowed to give him his medication, and he also needed extra care.

Shaun liked his new school, with Mr Philips his head master, he seemed to get on very well with him, He was there for a very long time and when a new school opened,

Living in Hope

nearer home, in Broxtowe, he had to move there, near to the swimming baths.

When Shaun was two years old, I lost a baby girl, and when Shaun was six years old we decided to try for a another baby, it was in 1972 when mark was born, a brother for Shaun,

I had an upsetting time over the birth of Mark, I had him by Caesarean when both our lives were at risk in Peel Street Hospital, Mark was christened in the chapel at the hospital and then was rushed to the special baby care unit, where he was kept in for two weeks I was kept in Peel street hospital for a week because I was too poorly, I could hear bells ringing and could see Angels and a bright light. I told the sister and she got the Doctor, she told me later that I had been dying and on my way to heaven, but God decided that I had to come back as my baby he would need me, I had not seen my new baby since he was born, and I was worried about him, and also our son Shaun at home, I was moved to a nursing home at St, Mary's for a week, which closed down when I was sent home.

On my way home I had to call and see my baby at the City Hospital, He was tiny, with blonde hair, he was lovely, but because he was so small, I had to be shown how to bath and dress him, I was scared of dropping him. When I finally got him home, I had to let him cry so his lungs would expand, I would lean over his crib, I could not hear him cry much he sounded like a kitten, but thank God he got stronger every day.

Margaret Plummer Russell

While all this was going on with Mark I still had to take Shaun, with his medication to the school bus every day and collect him every afternoon, but this gave me time with Mark.

Shaun really loved his baby brother and when Mark was christened in church he sat with Granddad and Mark on the settee looking after Mark for most of the time.

I also did work at home when the children were asleep to bring in extra money for holidays later I took a twilight job at Plessey 6 till 9pm Mike would look after the boys in the evening while I was at work, and I had them during the day it worked out well

It was better working twilight shift because I could put Shaun on the bus in the morning look after Mark and work on my allotment growing my own veg and fruit it also worked out better in the school holidays.

We had a good marriage, we could not have been happier, with two smashing boys, and a dog a Jack Russell, we were living in Leyton Crescent, Beeston where we had spent 25 years as a good Wife and Mother.

Mike had been in the Territorial Army and joined the Police as a special; he was in it for some years.

It was at this time, when I was at bingo, that Mike picked me up, and said that he had had a phone call from my brother Stephen and his wife Sheila, who lived in Barrow – in – Furness Cumbria.

He had left me his phone number and I phoned him as soon as I got home, this was the first time I had heard from any of my family for roughly 50 years.

Living in Hope

We arranged to go to Barrow to meet them, it was great and we stayed all weekend, Stephen and Sheila were so pleased to see us and the boys who they made very welcome Stephen and I were over the moon, it was great to have a 6ft brother to look up to after all this time, they also had a few stray cats.

They took us to Lake Windermere and when we got back Sheila made us a lovely dinner the first of many.

A few weeks later they came down to see us for the weekend, we took them to Nottingham and after tea we went for a walk down by the river. I really enjoyed having them down, but when they went home I really cried, I did not want them to go as I thought I would not see them again.

On other visits, we took them round Wollerton Hall as Sheila liked going round Stately Homes. I could not wait for the phone to ring again to say they where coming down to see us.

We went down to Barrow and we met Sheila Mum and dad and Stephens Adopted Parents, we all got on so well.

I remember Sheila telling me that her Mum worked for Ester Lauder and she gave me a bottle of perfume which I kept for special occasions as it smelt so lovely. It was the first present I had had from any of my family. Stephen and Sheila went to Spain and brought me a lovely musical piano and another time a black vase with figures on it.

Stephen told me that he had found our brother John who was married to Barbara and they had two children Judith and Robert and that he would take us up to see them They lived in a place called Accrington, he had also found two sisters that we did not know we had in Bury, their names were Pauline and Janie Some of the pieces of my past were falling back into place.

It was great to meet every one, and it made me so happy to see Mum and Dad again after all these years

I also met my brother Hughie my eldest brother, he flung his arms around me and nearly squeezed me to death, the only ones I had not met were my sister Margaret and brother James, but I new one day, with God's help, I would see them again.

Then my marriage went wrong, we got divorced, a lot of personal things went wrong- I did not think it would happen to me- I was so upset my world went upside down.

I went to court and came away with only 5 thousand pound and no where to live. Mike said that it was all he could afford, as he had taken up with another woman with children.

I put the money down on a house in Long Eaton as houses there were cheaper.

I had a house with a £ 5 thousand pound mortgage, the house had two bedrooms bathroom and a kitchen living room and a lounge with a long garden. It was all down to me now.

Living in Hope

The people needed a quick sale; I worked mornings at Plessey to pay the mortgage, so that the boys would always have a home to come to. and if it did not work out with me there was his Dad and his new woman.

I started going out with a man called Graham, and every thing was alright until I wanted to bring the boys home at week –ends, he did not and started getting violent and knocked me about, so I left him.

Mike married his second wife, who ill treated Mark, so I filed for custody of our two sons.Mark came to live with me first, followed by Shaun this meant three of us living in a two bedroom house so I had to move yet again, to Margaret Ave I believe that Shaun had been dragged out of a car and thrown against a brick wall, causing him to have a fit,-they knew he was Epileptic- and had put him in a top floor flat , in a rented house.

We were all happy in Margaret Ave, Shaun was working, and Mark was at secondary school, and I was working we managedSome time later I met Bill Rooney and he and the boys got on really well, we took the boys on holiday to Whitby, in a caravan. We bought the boys a Border collie which we called Jet, he was all black, with blue eyes and a pink nose.As he got older his feet and tip of his tail became white. His eyes changed to a lovely shade of brown his nose black.

Mark always wanted a Whippet or Greyhound and did not like Jet at first but they grew on each other, Jet followed Mark every where he went and Mark took Jet for walks when he came home from school.

At this time Bill was staying weekends with us, and Shaun working at Beeston, Shaun asked Bill if he could buy a house nearer to his work, and Bill and I said why not try, He asked us to help him and we said we would, he spotted a house in the Rylands and asked Bill and I to have a look at it Shaun liked it Bill said it was a good strong house, Bill managed to knock £2000 pounds off the asking price which made Shaun happy.

Shaun got the house and was really happy; it was what he had always wanted.

When Shaun had moved into his own house Mike kept paying his maintenance late, and it put me into arrears with my mortgage, money was very tight, Shaun said to come and live with him and bring Mark to and the dog, so I sold up and moved in with Shaun.

I stayed there for two years but I still wanted my own house, but could not afford it.

CHAPTER 6
ACCRINGTON

I went to visit my Brother John in Accrington, the houses were a lot cheaper there, Bill and I were thinking of moving up there and asked Shaun to come with us but Shaun said he had a good job and did not want move.

We found a house Chester Street Accrington and paid cash from the last house I was to move in and Bill was to follow me later.

I had a part grant on the house and it turned out quite well.

While I was in Accrington Bill told me that he could not move in as his Mother had become very ill we did not know at the time she had Cancer of the colon.

We went through a bad patch, not knowing where our relationship was going until Bill said his Mum was going into a Warden Controlled flat, Bill was working full time and did not like leaving his Mum on her own and as her friends had moved in to the flats she would have someone to go to the local shops with.

The worst was to come she took very ill after a couple of years in the flat she had to go into hospital and was in for thirteen weeks and died in hospital, I did all I could to help Bill through this awful time.

As she was dying I was asked took look after Bill which I promised to do.

Bill was left the house in Silverdale, Nottingham so he asked me to move in with him.

While I was living with Shaun, Mark went in the Army at 16 years of age and came out when he was 17,years old over a girl we had some problems with Mark and I had to tell him to leave and go and live with his dad He ended up on the Streets, so I moved back to Nottingham to try and find him and give him a home which he did , but shortly after he moved to Spain as a chef, and I finally moved in with Bill and live in the Bungalow where we live now

CHAPTER 7
NOTTINGHAM-AGAIN

Then something happened , that I had wanted for such a long time, While I was Bingo, Margaret had phoned and spoken to bill, and had said she had been looking for me for many years, When I came home I phoned Margaret right away, I new her voice it was great talking to her after all this time.

I had told Bill about Margaret and our early lives together as Bill and I had planned to go to Scotland for two weeks when we got back we went straight up to Liverpool to see my sister Margaret on the following Saturday.

When we got to Margaret s home my nieces Gaynor and Sue and their children Gemma and Aimee, and their Husbands Neville and Kevin and Margaret's husband Tom were all there

It was hugs and Kisses all round with tears of happiness, I felt as though I knew Tom with talking on the phone to him.

Tom and Margaret took us all over Liverpool I showed Bill where I used to live at Woodbine Street and we saw the Eternal Flame that burns at Liverpool football ground, it brought back a lot of happy memories also the Liver Buildings and the Ferries crossing the Mersey.

Margaret Plummer Russell

All this happened in the August we only had to find our brother James as we had planned a re-union in Ramsbottom and up till then he was the only one we had not found.

But on the 19th October Margaret phoned me and said we had traced James and as it turned out it was also his birthday Margaret gave me his phone number and I spoke to James for the first time in over 56 years he told me he had two Daughters Jane and Joanne and three Grand children. We seemed to talk for ever as we had a lot of time to make up.

We had the re-union at the Rose and Crown, in Ramsbottom it was a very moving time for all of us and one that I would not have missed. The next summer James and his wife Sandra came and spent a week with us we took them to Buxton and other places and enjoyed it so much I didn't want them to go. While Jimmy was here he told me he had been fishing in the River Trent on many a weekend he had been so close and we did not know.

Then the worst thing in my life happened, my son Shaun died on the 26th of March 2003 with Epilepsy. Shaun was only 38 years old and had every thing to live for; it was funny how things worked out, with the family meeting up again when I needed all the help in the world. Margaret came down for a few days as soon as she heard. It meant a lot to me and I really appreciated it. Bill was great through it all and stood by Margaret and I.

Living in Hope

Shaun Dad and his wife Barbara came to the funeral along with all my family.

I have had a lot of things go wrong in my life, but have always been able to get up and carry on. But losing Shaun has taken every thing out of me and I need Gods help to give me strength to carry on.

Bev my counsellor has given me a lot of help to get through.

I also lost my eldest brother Hugh who we cremated on the Tuesday and Shaun on the Friday my brother Johns foster brother Allan was also cremated on the Tuesday.

My life has changed I feel as though a piece of me has died I looked after Shaun all his life and he had been the best son any one could have, he had to fight for every day of his life to live so I must carry on and not let him down it will be very hard.

I thank Fred and Linda for all the Godly help they gave to me.

The Club gave Shaun a good send of after the cremation he had helped at the Club for quite a few years the club have now put up a plaque with his name on for all the hard work and hours he put in on the lighting system and Bingo God Bless Shaun till we meet again.

Now my life is going to be spent with Bill and my son mark my two dogs and my long lost familyBefore I finish my story our son Mark and his wife Wendy presented us with a beautiful gift, a granddaughter Masie, our family is now complete,

*Jericho Workhouse Bury. Recent Photo.
To where the children were taken into care*

Duck Pond Buckhurst

Chapel/School (Buckhurst) from where Margaret was taken into care

Minster Lodge (Ormiskirk) Children's Home

Margaret – Frst time in St Paul's Church Ramsbottom where all children were christened and Hugh's burial service was held

Cliffe Nursing Home <ref Hugh's story>

Margaret (tallest), Lilian (foster sister), Mr and Mrs Dean (foster parents). Bootle, Liverpool

Margaret at Mum's grave. Ramsbottom Cemetary

Closes Cottage after recent modernisation from where the children were taken

*Mum, Margaret and Hugh as young children,
Uncle Bill (not Dad) about 1940*

Aunt Alice House <ref Margaret and James>

Kirkham Children's Home (Margaret and Alice)

Part 5
James' Story

Chapter 1

James in 1950 aged 7

This is the story of a family that was torn apart back in 1949.

A family of eight in all, mum dad and six siblings. I am the fourth child in this family. The oldest brother Hugh, Sisters Margaret and Alice, and my-self James, then John and Stephen.

What was to happen to us all later we did not know or why, and would not find out till years later in 2001.

As I start my story, it fills me with sadness knowing, we, as a family were not to grow up to-gether. We were separated as children from our parents because of illness and lack of money. Back in them days if you didn't work then there was no money coming into the house. For some reason our father left us, and mum was left alone to bring us up. She could not work so how was she to feed us. When mum went into Hospital to have Stephen, our oldest sister Margaret took care of us the best way she could, but as she was only young her-self, how was she to do it. Shortly after mum brought Stephen home from hospital, that's when the authorities came and started to take us children away.

I was born on Fir Street on the Peel Brow estate in Ramsbottom on the 19th October 1943.

My mother was Margaret Russell nee Kenyon my father Hugh Russell I had an older brother and two sisters. I remember my sister Margaret used to push me around the estate in my pram. Two years later, on 26th October 1945, our brother John was born. Time to change places in the pram, John at the top, me sat at the bottom. There was four pre-fab houses just out side our house, one at each corner in a square. Margaret would push us around the square till we were dizzy.

Later we moved to a cottage at Buckhurst, Nangreeves. There were two little cottages together; our family in one and an old gentleman lived in the other.

I cannot remember our father being at the cottage with us just mum. Our brother Stephen was born on 9th October 1948 while still living at the cottage.

There was a little school, come Sunday school, close by but not many pupils attended, just children from surrounding farms and cottages that dotted around the moors.

There was a small stream that ran by the cottage that resembled a mini waterfall that ran into a pool with a small bridge across it. We crossed this bridge to get to the cottage. It was a very quiet place; you could hear the wild fowl calling to one another over the moors. The old man that lived next door had some geese, and every time I went over the bridge they would chase, me and peck my legs and backside. In my mind I can still hear the sound of the wind, and the stream as it went over the waterfall that ended in the pool.

The peace we once had as a family was soon to be torn apart. At the time I was too young to know what or why this was to happen to us. It was years later we were to find out. Our mum went into hospital to have Stephen, so our sister Margaret took care of us the best way she could. When mum came home from hospital after having Stephen, Margaret still took care of us, some days she missed going to school. When she returned to school, a woman came and told Margaret she was going on a holiday, but she was taken to a workhouse in Jericho near Bury.

Shortly after the rest of us were to join her, but for Hugh who ran away, but he was soon found and joined us at the workhouse.

Margaret was then told again she was going on holiday, I said" me come to, Margaret", but the women said "no, you have to stay here" but my sister said" I will come back for you James. A part of me went with her that day, and it was to be over fifty years before I saw my sister again. I never forgot my sister Margaret.

Alice John, and Stephen, were then taken, where to I did not know. Hugh and I where taken to a children's home, where Hugh ran away a few times, but was always found and brought back. Later, on the 10th of December 1949 we were sent to Atherleigh children's home. We spent about four months there, and when Hugh was old enough to leave, he would not leave me there alone, so he took me to mum's sister Auntie Alice at 5 Mount Street, Ramsbottom.

Hugh went into the Army to do his National service. Even though Auntie Alice had two children of her own, Fred and Jean and no husband (he died young due to an accident at work) she took me in and I was treated like one of the family.

On 17th April 1950 I started at Holcombe Infants School. I can remember my school days. It was a good School, but being the smallest there I was picked on quite a bit, but eventually one by one I got them back. Mrs Parkinson was head teacher then, and she would give some of us little errands to do after our dinner.

I was sent to a Joiners shop, where the man kept pigs, with any left over food from the dinners I was given a packet of sweets in return for pig food. On Thursday's it was saving day, and the children would bring money into school to put into saving's club. Mine was three pennies; it was then taken to post office in the village.

Aunty Alice took me to Blackpool, but I cannot remember getting money from savings club.

Living in Hope

Then there was the Whit walk, from the school down to Holcombe brook and back up to the sanatorium, where we would have a run about before going back to School.

I still saw my Brother Hugh when he came home on leave.

He re-enlisted and I did not see him again till many years later in 2001.

I remember the Gaslights in Aunty Alice's

House with a mantle on, and you had to light it first, with

a match, then turn the gas on. The light was not as bright as

Electric, but still a good light. When the mantle burnt out

I had to run down to the corner shop, to get another one.

Then straight back home, but we still had a stock of candles,

in the cupboard, in case the gas went off.

After tea I would go out playing and when the gaslights in the street came on, I would climb the lamp-post and switch them off again, and run like mad.

There was this old air-raid shelter on the way to Holcombe at Rake Fold where we used to hide. We took orange boxes to sit on, and of course our comics, the Beano and Eagle to read. We also lit a fire in the shelter, so we could put potatoes in to bake them, then we could eat them when they were ready. But just below the shelter was a row of houses, so we had to be careful not to be seen, or the police would be sent for. Like one night I did cause a big bang. I put a tin of beans on the fire, and it went off with an almighty bang. All the people in houses came out to see what the noise was all about, just as we came out of the shelter, covered in beans. We didn't go there again for a long time after that night.

On Saturday afternoons, when we had done all our jobs, I and some mates would go over to the tip at Hazle Hurst on our bikes, to see if there were any old bikes that had been thrown away. If we found any, we would take parts off them that we wanted, tyres and such, we'd take them home and change our bikes around. I had a lot of lights on my bike, more lights than on Christmas tree in the middle of Ramsbottom at Christmas time. I once found an old bike, with an engine in the back wheel. I messed about with it, and got it going. You had to peddle it to get it going; it lasted about four weeks till it blew the back wheel off. Back to old bike.

Aunty Alice would play hell with me for having too much scrap in the out-house. There was no room for dolly tub, mangle and scrubbing board, that was used on wash days, and of course the old tin bath. So it was off to tip once again with all scrap I'd collected. On washdays, out would come dolly tub scrubbing board and posser, and I helped Aunty Alice do all washing.

Later when we got electricity, Aunty was able to buy a twin tub washing machine, so washing day was a lot easier then.

Living in Hope

Then there was shopping day, so off to the shops we go. They were brown paper carrier bags then, with string handles that cut into your fingers, especially when it was full of spuds, (potatoes). I carried, half dragged them up the hill as they were that heavy.

Ration books came into force then, and shop keeper's took out the stamps to pay for food. On Brook Bond tea, there was a stamp on the front of the packet that was worth a penny. These stamps were saved by sticking them onto a saving card, and when card was full it could be redeemed towards the shopping.

When weather was bad, and couldn't go out to play Aunty would cut up old clothes to make a rag rug for in front of fire. I would pass her colour's she wanted, and she would thread them through a piece of old sacking to make different patterns. Aunty always made her own rugs for in front of fire, as coal would fall out of fire and scorch them.

In 1954 I was eleven, time for the high school. It was hard at first to get used to the bigger school, having to make new friend's, and a lot more subjects to learn. Much more classroom's too. It was a big jump from the three rooms at the infant school; also we had to make a time table out, so we knew which class we had to go to next, and we had homework to do.

At the end of each day I would run home to get thing's ready for tea, peel spuds, and butter bread, get tea pot ready so when Aunty came home she could finish off the tea.

To get a bit of extra pocket money, I found an evening's and weekend job on a farm, helping to milk cows, and collect the eggs. All the eggs had to be cleaned, using a damp cloth, then packed into boxes.

The milk was put into aluminium kit's, with pint and half pint measuring ladles attached to the side. The people would come out with jugs for the milk, and cloth's to place on top of jug's to keep fly's out. The money I earned was thirty shilling (one pound fifty pence). It was hard work, but I liked it. Aunty Alice never had to buy eggs or milk.

On Saturday night it was off to local picture house with fish and chip's to eat on way home.

Aunty Alice worked in the cotton mill, and I remember the sound her clogs made on the flags at the front of the house.

Like many more who worked in the cotton mills, the sound of their clog's faded as they went down the streets to the bottom of town.

We did not have toilets in the house, they were in the back yard, and in winter we put an old jacket under the door to keep out draughts, The toilet paper was old newspapers cut up into squares and hung on back of the door on a nail. I once set fire to the paper to keep warm, but the smell of the smoke had Aunty Alice running up the yard with a bucket of water thinking id set fire to the toilet. She opened the door and threw the water in wetting me through, it was ice cold too. I sat there

Living in Hope

shivering, with my teeth chattering, and then got sent to bed without a jam butty.

It was also my job to get the fire lit for when Aunty came home from work. To get the coal to catch, I" put a shovel up to fireplace, with a piece of newspaper in front, to get it to draw. Sometimes the dam paper would catch fire, and I" have to run around the house, opening windows, to get rid of smoke before Aunty Alice got in.

When I was at Peel Brow High School, every Wednesday dinnertime, I ran down Fir Street, past the hen pens, to Kenyon Street, to the cotton mill where Aunty Alice and her daughter Jean worked. Across from the mill was a little chip shop, and I'd go in and get pie and peas for our dinner. By the time I got there it was dinnertime, so the machines would stop, and we sat in between them to eat our dinner. Then back to school for me.

The soap works was at the bottom end of Kenyon Street, and a lad I knew at school, his dad worked there and would give me soap flakes and bars of soap to take home.

On Friday's, Aunty would call in cake shop, on Bridge Street, to get some potted beef and oven bottom muffins, for our tea.

Sunday's was baking day, and Aunty would bake meat and potato, and apple and rhubarb, pies for tea. They were good, and better than shop bought ones,

Aunty Alice would lift washing out to put through mangle, I would turn the handle for her, and the mangle squeezed all water out of washing..

When I was fifteen, I left school to start work in Presswell Cotton Mill, that was just behind the picture house. In them days, you could get a job straight from school, and mine was in the cotton industry.

I learnt quite a lot about how a bale of cotton was broken down to the finished article. Trucks would come to the factory loaded with bales of cotton, and be unloaded into the warehouse, where it would be broken down in the machine where soap would be added to stop it drying out. Then it went into the card room, where it was spun into rope like coils. The Darby would spin it lightly, before going into the mule room. Mule spinning consisted of five or six hundred bobbins being spun at the same time. The bobbins would then be sent to different parts of the mill to be spun into cotton to weave hand and bath towels. The finer tread would be woven for curtains and clothing.

I left the mill to work in the colliery, but that closed down, so I got a job in coal yard, back in Ramsbottom. This job was ok, but you got wet through a lot, especially in winter. It was that cold, and frosty, it would make your hands crack, and bleed it was very sore, and painful too. We would wear mittens to help the cracks to heal. Trudging through snow, and around back streets over icy cobbles, and sometimes slipping over with sacks of coal, on your back was hard work. Sometimes we were ask if

Living in Hope

we wanted a cup of tea by the old folk. but we had no time to stop for tea, we had to get work done, then off home to get dried out. By the time day was over, I knew I had done a days work.

After a while I decided to have a change so I got a job at Turnbulls and Stockdales in Stubbins. They got cloth from all over the country, silk and satin for printing on. Turnbulls had four mills. At the Chaderton weaving mill, they stretched the cloth to make it wider. Ewood lane mill, was used for the warehouse and dispatch. The main one was where I worked, mixing different colours, sometimes twenty or thirty different colours per pattern. There were thirty or more printing machines on one floor. The top floor was for block printing on tables some fifty foot long and five foot wide. By the time you had done one table pattern you could have handled some two hundred print blocks for just one pattern. There was screen-printing too but I didn't do any of that.

I finished at Turnbulls and went into learning catering in Ramsbottom. As the job was long hours, I left Aunty Alice's and lived in flat above the shop. The back of the shop was for cooking the meat. My job was to deliver all the supplies to all the canteens, and three times a week I would go to the market in Bolton, for fresh vegetables, and the slaughterhouse for meat.

Once I'd supplied the canteens with what they needed, then I would start the cooking for evening functions, sometimes it would be very late nights. The hardest was the agricultural shows at Bury and Great Harwood, and the police Balls at King George hall in Blackburn. Hundreds of people came from all over the district.

In early 1968, while still working in catering, I met a girl called Sandra, on a blind date. I then left Ramsbottom to live in Todmorden where Sandra lived. She was working in the cotton industry, at Mons Mill in Todmorden so I got a job there too.

Then twelve month later on the 1st of March 1969 we were married. I left the mill to work at Sandholm Iron Company the week before we married; then the week after Mons Mill was going to close down.

We lived at first in a one up one down house, with a small kitchen partitioned off in one corner of the front room.

On the 4th April 1970 our first daughter, Joanne was born.

The following year on 3rd March 1971 our second daughter Jane was born.

When the girl's got older they started to ask questions, why they had no grandparents, aunties, or uncles on my side of the family. I could only tell them what I could remember at that time- that I had an older brother and sister, and a younger brother. The only name I could remember was my older sister Margaret. I could not remember my mum, or dad. As far as I knew they had died when I was young.

Years later they asked about tracing my family, but we kept coming up against a brick wall.

Why?

Because un-be known to me, they were all called Russell I was Hardman even though my father was Hugh Russell and mother was Margaret Russell my surname is Hardman, I still don't know why.

As my youngest daughter had a computer, she said we could try looking on it to see if we could find my family, but the brick wall came again.

Then one day out of the blue a knock came at the door. As I opened it, somehow I knew it was my brother. He said, "Hello are you James?"

I replied "yes, and I think you are my brother". He said "yes, I am your brother John".

I am not very good on my feet, but that day I had wings, my wife Sandra was up-stairs. I could not get there quick enough to shout, "My brother is at the door" she came running down two at a time saying, "what did you say". I repeated "my brother John is at the door". What a surprise, my younger brother to arrive on my birthday of all days.19th October 2001. That day will never be forgotten. It was a very special birthday present that year. He came with his daughter Judith and her two sons. It was Judith that found me. We had a good chat before they had to leave. He informed me on how they traced me, and that they had found all family now, and said how I had an older sister and younger brother that I had not remembered. I was apparently the last one they found.

CHAPTER 2
REUNION

John and Margaret had arranged a reunion at the Rose and Crown public house in Ramsbottom so that all the family could get together. My wife my girls, grandchildren and I were that excited after all this time we were finally going to meet my long lost family. We did lose some sleep over the next few weeks waiting for that day to arrive. Maybe now I can find out what happened to us all those years ago?.

When we arrived at the Rose and Crown car park, I was getting out of the car and there was this woman looking across at me. As I looked at her, thinking "I know you from somewhere", she came over and said, "I know you, your Jimmy," "that's right" I replied. She then said "You used to play with my brother Ralph, when you were kids. I'm his older sister Sheila", I had only been back in Ramsbottom two minutes, and already met someone from my past.

Then I turned around, and there was my sister Alice. She had travelled down with her partner Bill, and son Shaun from Nottingham. They had come in their camper van so they could stay over night.

Then my young brother Stephen arrived whom I had not seen since he was a baby. Strange how the first two

Living in Hope

to arrive were the ones I'd forgotten about until John had reminded me of them.

After we shook hands and hugged one another we made our way into the pub.

We were the first ones to arrive. I was standing at the bar getting another drink when the door opened and in walked my sister Margaret. Even after all these years I knew it was my sister standing there. She almost dropped the large cake she was holding when she saw me, as she also knew it was me standing there. The sister I had lost some fifty years ago at the workhouse in Jericho. That piece of me that had gone with her all those years ago was back. I don't think I had a tear left, but they were tears of joy at seeing my sister again. Then John and his family walked in, they had called for my older brother Hugh, but they found him ill so he could not come. There was also two half- sisters I didn't know about, Janie and Pauline, but Janie wasn't able to come, and Pauline unfortunately had died some years ago of cancer. It was really nice to see them all and get to know one another again.

We were also lucky enough to meet the chap who now lives in the house that Aunty Alice once lived in. and also where I grew up. The chap called Graham, very kindly invited us all up to the house in Mount Street. So every one of us walked up the road, then the alley, that leads to Mount Street. Graham was very interested in our family and how we all came to be split up.I still knew the way, and the memories came flooding back as soon as I walked into that house. The old pantry wall had been taken down, and no closet under the stairs and even the toilet in the back yard had gone. But to me it was still the same old house.

Some of the neighbours, who were there when I was a lad, were still living there. Who also remembered me too. So we had a good old chinwag about the past. Then we went up the back to a special place of mine, the woods we used to play in. The big oak tree is still there that we used to swing on. We will be going back to see Graham to tell him how things are going and thank him for that special day he gave to every one of us.

A couple of weeks later my wife and I went back to Mount Street to see another neighbour who was away at the time of the reunion called Norma. She lived two doors away from where Aunty Alice had lived, and she had two boys younger than me, but they used to follow me all around. I enjoyed taking them with me to play, and sometimes I would sit on the doorstep, with them, and many a time they would come into Aunty Alice's for a biscuit or two.

Norma was a good friend to Aunty Alice and also knew mum. She told us a lot about the family and how mum regularly came to visit, but I don't remember seeing her.

If I had, I would not have known it was my mum, as Aunty Alice never talked to me about her. Another friend of Aunty Alice was a Mrs Savage; they used to take me to the pictures on a Friday night, and I remember two sweet shops I would go, in one for two ounces of peanuts. After

Living in Hope

the pictures we would have a bag of chips to share on the way home.

A Mr Willits, lived next door, and sometimes I would help in the garden turning the soil over and dig up the vegetables. His son Jack was a cobbler in town on Bridge Street He repaired my shoes for nothing for helping his dad with the garden.

Seeing Norma again brought this all back to me and more. She told me about George Hardman, the second father. He used to work in the steel factory, in Bury, till he lost the job. With what money he had, he bought a horse and cart and went around collecting rags and anything that people threw out.

A rag and bone man, they used to call them in those days. In payment for rags you would get a donkey stone to clean your front doorstep or a dolly blue for the washing, to make it whiter. He later got the name of Packie Hardman. Whatever money he made that day, he would go into the nearest pub and drink till all the money had gone. Not one penny left to give mum for food or anything, just drank it all away. George Hardman came on the scene around 1949 or 1950. He is not my father, but I have his name. Why? --I don't know. My brother Hugh has since told us how one day he went round to mums, and as he walked in the door, George Hardman was belting one of the girls on the stairs. Hugh picked him up and said," If I ever catch you hitting one of the girls again, I will hit you."

We now know mum and George Hardman had another family after she lost us, two girls Janie and Pauline.

I was to meet my brother Hugh again for the first time in over fifty years. Margaret and her husband Tom came over from Liverpool, to take us over to his flat in Bury. I did not know what to expect after all these years, but was very pleased to be seeing him again. Just to be able to talk to him about what happened to us was, at the time enough for me. But Hugh was not in good health, he had diabetes. He also could not see very well. He knew who I was though, and was glad I had called on him. The more we saw of him, the more he told us about the past.

Hugh had a very good neighbour, called Pat, who called in every day, to see him; and one day when she called, he was on the floor, he had collapsed. He was taken to Fairfield Hospital in Bury. Hugh had suffered a stroke; the doctor asked us if the worst came to the worst would we want him resuscitated.

What a decision to make.

We could not decide there and then as rest of family had to be told. But it was left to Margaret and myself to make that decision.

To think after all these years apart and to only just find him, only to lose him again. To lose him now would leave a big hole in our hearts. But Hugh started to improve and we visited him as often as we could. We tried to alternate our visits so there was always one of us there to help him recover. Then came the time where the Hospital could

Living in Hope

do no more for him, and he could not go back to living alone as he could not look after himself. So we had to start looking for a nursing home for him. Eventually after days of phone calls and running around, a care home was found in Stubbins at Ramsbottom. That was where Hugh wished to go, back to his home town.

The Nursing home was once the Porrit family's home, who owned the cotton mill in Stubbins. A lovely big house with gardens all the way around it. We mentioned this home to Hugh's social worker, and with-in a couple of day's Hugh was taken there. Only we were not informed until he was about to be moved.

Hugh had a nice big room, with views over Edenfield and the lovely garden.

We had some very good times when we visited Hugh, and that was as often as we could. We would chat about the old days, and try to piece together what happened when we all got split up.

He was always happy to see us, Margaret was the first to go into his room, and a big smile would come on his face, then the tears would come. Mostly because he thought we hadn't been to see him for a long time. Sometimes he would be sad and ask for grandma and Aunty Alice. Because of his condition he didn't realise they had died years before. Then we would get out the bag of sweets, and he heard the paper rattling he would give us a big smile and say "ha sweeties, come on then share them out." Tom and I never got a look in. Hugh loved his sweets, pork pies too, but was only allowed them now and again because of his diabetes.

I remember one weekend when we went to visit Hugh it was a bright summer's day. We asked Hugh if he would like to go outside to sit in the sun and see the garden, so the staff got him dressed to go out in the wheelchair. He wasn't all that keen, when he got out, because he cursed to go back in. So we took him into the dinning room, where we chatted about all sorts of things, as Hugh said, he remembered going passed the house to get to the moors. Hugh then said go and look for my motorbike I left in the bushes.

We think he was a bit confused, but looked anyway. He was much better when we took him back to his room. He would ask about his cats, as he was very attached to them. He missed them too. So we asked him if he would like us to bring them in so he could see they were well looked after. The biggest smile came on his face, the staff agreed to let us take in the cats.

So on our next visit that is what we did. As soon as he heard them his eyes lit up, with a big smile on his face, it was worth its weight in gold to see that.

Hugh had problems with eyesight, and had difficulties seeing us. So Margaret and I decided to see his doctor to ask if there was anything that could be done to improve his sight. The doctor said he could try laser treatment to give him a bit more vision. So an appointment was made for him to visit Birch hill Hospital. It was very tiring for Hugh though sitting in wheelchair waiting to be seen,

Living in Hope

he kept slipping down and we kept lifting him back up. He would get very agitated and swear at us. But I think in back of his mind he knew we would always be there for him no matter what. Margaret and Tom would come all the way from Liverpool to the home so she could be with him in the ambulance. Tom would then go to the hospital where I would meet him there.

Hugh had quite a few trips there over the next few months, till there was nothing more they could do for him. The treatment only gave him a bit more sight but he was happy with that. When we next visited Hugh in the home we asked the sister in charge if there was any possibility that Hugh would ever go back home to his flat, but the answer was no as he would need twenty four hour care. He would not be able to look after himself like he had in the past.

This was a heart breaking time for us all, as his little flat had to be emptied It was his home, his independence. That was all being taken away from him.

Some of his belongings were taken to the nursing home, that he could have in his own room. His personal things, we took care of, as they could not be kept in the home, what was left went to the local charity shop. His two cats fluffy and tinker what was to happen to them? Then my wife said, look, we will take the cats in for now, until a good home can be found for them. But in the end she could not let them go, it was the one thing we could do for Hugh to look after his cats. Now them cats are a part of our lives, and through them we still have a part of Hugh in our life.

Then out of the blue came a shock, none of us were expecting. Hugh had taken a turn for the worse he was very ill and was once again taken into Hospital. The sister in charge at the nursing home rang Margaret to let her know, she then contacted me so we could all be with him at the Hospital. We were told Hugh had a bad chest infection and this caused renal failure and pneumonia, they did not give us much hope for our brother Hugh. We visited him every day for the next couple of weeks Then I was asked about Hugh being put on a pathway to let him slip away peacefully, and without any more pain or suffering. Two days later Margaret got a phone call to say our Hugh had died early that morning. The 25th may 2003 Aged 67. The funeral was held at Saint Paul's church in Ramsbottom on the 3rd of June 2003. The vicar game a lovely service fit for the gentleman that he was. His army regiment, The Lancashire Fusiliers, sent two standard bearers and two from the Royal British legion. The rest of the service was held at Accrington crematorium. We only had the last two years with Hugh to get to know him again and the memories of our time together will always be with us. Our brother Hugh is going to be very sadly missed by us all

CHAPTER 3
REVISITS

I can still see Ramsbottom as it was some fifty years ago, back when I lived there as a lad. I have revisited on a number of occasions, and also been to see the infant school at Holcombe that I went to as a lad. It looks just the same apart from the office that is now built onto the side. Margaret, Tom and I went, as I wanted to see if there were any records of me when I was there. Mr Beadie is head master there now, and made us very welcome. He showed us around the classrooms, then we went into his office where he showed us some records of when I attended the school in 1950, at the age of seven. Mr Beadie also had some photographs of children that year, but I didn't recognise any of them. I remember a Mrs Parkinson was head mistress then and the caretaker was Mr Hanker, his wife was the dinner lady. The village of Holcombe is still the same as it was, with the church near the school. I remember how people used to come to Holcombe village to watch the fox hunt, outside the local pub that stands back from the road. All the Huntsmen and Hounds, what a sight it was to see.

I left Holcombe School in 1954 to go to the High School at Peel Brow. But sadly I can't visit the School, as it's been pulled down to make way for a motorway.

Margaret, Tom, Sandra and I walked down Kenyon Street where our Aunty Alice once worked in the cotton mill. There are no rows of houses opposite the mill that once lined the Street, they have all been pulled down to make way a for a re-cycling plant. The railway is there still. I remember pulling the trucks along the platform and how the porter would chase me off.

There is no waiting room or parcel office, in the station now and the bus depot as gone. Where the fire station is now, that used to be sidings for coal yard. Steam trains would shunt their coal wagons down to the station then back to the coal yard. The Grants Arms public house is still there it had gardens at the front though and a little shelter. This was where they used to hold the carol service around the Christmas tree. The entire garden was lit up with fairy lights. Even though there are a lot of changes in Ramsbottom its still the lovely valley that I grew up in.

I tell my Grandchildren the antics I got up to as a kid, how I climbed apple and pear trees, and take the risk of getting caught and getting smacked for riding our bikes down the hill without brakes and smashing into walls. I once took a sheet off a washing line on Halloween night, I made arrangements to meet my mates in the churchyard at Holcombe, it was pitch black as I laid on top of this big grave stone, I could hear my mates shout for me, so I shouted back I'm hear over by the angel. At that moment, the cloud that was covering the moon passed to reveal the moonlight, so as my mates passed

Living in Hope

I gave a low groan and sat up with the sheet over my head. They set off running, you couldn't see them for dust. I could do nothing for laughing. Sometimes, I used to go across to the farm at the end of our Street to help clean out the cow shed, I enjoyed that. The farmer would get turnips for the cows, so I would take some home to share with people on our Street As time went past and autumn came around, and on the way home from school down the winding road, this old man would sweep up all the leaves into little piles, and we would kick them all over the place. He would then sweep them all up again, and later we would set fire to them and cause loads of smoke.

Even now, when I smell smoke, burning leaves, or grass, I think of the good old times growing up. Sometimes the postman with his van would be taking the mail up to the village, he would give us a lift, stopping on his way to either deliver the mail or pick it up from out of the mail boxes in the wall. Then came bonfire time, we would start gathering wood, paper, just about anything that would burn. We would knock on doors to ask if they had anything they wanted rid of for our bonfire, as there was always someone who wanted rid of their old furniture or rubbish. We would go into the woods at the back of Aunty Alice's and cut branches off the trees.

We had our bonfire on the big lawn at the front of the house's, about fifty yards away from the front doors. Mrs Howarth who lived on our Street would come out and say " that bonfire is too big it will set fire to our entire house's". "Great" we said "then we would have a bigger bonfire." So out came the yard brush that she would clout us with, if she could catch us. It didn't make any difference though the rubbish kept on coming. Tyres, boxes, even the fencing that was not nailed down would make our bonfire bigger. We would make a guy Fawkes out of a pair of old trousers and shirt that we would stuff with old newspapers, that was our Guy for the top of bonfire. Then we would go around the houses singing penny for the Guy. Some people would give us sweets or biscuits but mostly a penny or two.

What money we collected ,Aunty Alice would save till nearer the time, and she would buy the fire works for us. All the neighbours would make parkin, toffee apples, and bonfire toffee. We put potatoes in the fire to bake them, I think we were eating charcoal half the time. But every-body apart from grumpy old Mrs Howarth had a real good night.

The day after, we would all get to-gether, to clean up all what was left of the bonfire so it was all clean and tidy again. That was a fun day too as what had not burnt we set fire to again. While out collecting wood for our bonfire, I would get some smacks from Aunty Alice, for climbing the trees and ripping the backside out of me trousers, I then got the nick name of "Jimmy and his magic patch". I have now come to the end of my story, of being separated from my family and growing up without my sisters and brothers, believing my parents had died when I was young.

Living in Hope

Knowing that my sister Margaret who looked after me had been taken away, where to I did not know. But now we are all back together again. But sadly we did not get enough time with our brother Hugh, who passed away in 2003. We now know what happened all those years ago and why. Tears of joy and heart ache have been shed at finding out what happened to us all, but now we can put that all behind us, and make the most of what time we have left with one another and the future is much brighter.

We visit one another as often as we can and chat on the phone trying to make up for lost time. Since finding my family and going back to Ramsbottom my mind has been opened up, its as if I pushed everything into a black hole in the back of my mind and now it has all come flooding back.

There is one thing id liked to have been able to do and that is to thank my Aunty Alice for taking me in and looking after me as one of her own children. She was really good to me despite the fact that her own children were much older than I was. She really did her best for me. I lost touch with her and her children when I moved from Ramsbottom and they were unable to find me, to let me know Aunty Alice had died

It was Margaret who found out what happened to the family years ago. She painstakingly looked through the archives in bury. When our father left us in the mid nineteen forties and our grandparents had died mum took over there house on Fi street that is when things started to go down hill. Having no one to look after us so she could go to work there was no money coming into the house. How was she to pay the rent, couldn't she got behind with the payment's. That's when the Authorities came and mum was told we would be evicted if payments were not made. Then George Hardman came on the scene and things went from bad to worse he found the cottage at Buckhurst and moved us in there. A lot of the time he was around and still no money coming in. Then after Stephen was born the Authorities came again to find all us children were neglected. That's when we were all taken away, one by one. Later our mum and George Hardman were taken to court and sent to prison for six month for neglecting us six children.
Our father Hugh Russell went on to have another family and was found to have lived in Burnley in Lancashire, where he died on 21-2- 1960. After mum was released from prison she tried to get us Children back but because of ill health she was refused. She didn't want any of us to be adopted but after a long battle with Stephen's foster parents she agreed to let them adopt him. The rest of us remained Fostered. Then later mum and George Hardman went on to have another family two daughters Janie and Pauline.

Part 6
John's Story

CHAPTER 1
ACCRINGTON

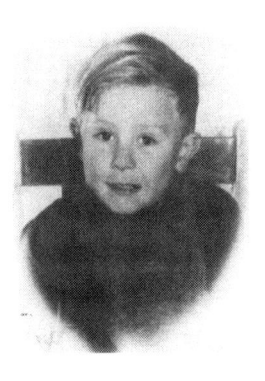

John in 1954 aged 4.

I was born on the 26th October 1945, at 63 Fir Street, Ramsbottom, as were my sister Alice, and my brother James.

I have no memories of my early life before I was 3 years old, when I was placed with my foster parents—Ivy and Wilf Caple-- in 1949, in Accrington. I lived with them until my marriage in 1969.

Ivy and Wilf already had a son, Alan, who was 3 years older than me, and there was Albert, (my mum's father). I can remember playing "buses", with him, where we used to line up all the stand chairs. Granddad would be the driver, Alan and I would be the passengers and mum would be the conductress.

Alan and I went to Benjamin Hargreaves Primary school in Plantation Street, Accrington.

One day when we came home from school, Granddad had died. They laid him out in his coffin in the front room at home, until his funeral. The funeral service was at Wesley church, which I attended until I was fourteen years old. Mum and Dad attended three times each Sunday.

My Granddad was chauffer to Sir Alfred McAlpine, famous for McAlpine Construction, I missed him very much, he was always playing games with us.

Shortly after, we moved from Sandy lane to Augusta street. This meant that I had to change schools, and I went to St Mary's which was only two streets away.

I did quite well at school and should have taken my 11 plus exam , but I did not tell my mum and missed the exam.

During my early years I was known as John Caple, but as I got older I wanted to keep my family name of Russell, in the hope that one day my family would find me.

My mum and dad(Ivy and Wilf) told me what they knew of my life before I came to live with them.

When I arrived at their home I was asked what I wanted to eat. I always said "crisps and pop" which is all I would eat for quite awhile.

They also told me that I had been taken away from my parents when I was two years old, along with several brothers and sisters and put into a children's home- somewhere.?

I was with a brother, and the family who took my brother, had only wanted one child, so they took the baby. I was left in the home until Ivy and Wilf asked the Methodist church for a little boy to live with them, as a brother for their only son, Alan.

Ivy and Wilf were strict but fair, and we were brought up well. We enjoyed caravan holidays all over the country.

I left school at 15 and became an apprentice baker which I thoroughly enjoyed. During my college years I was second out of over two hundred entrants for baking Turog bread, we actually made Hovis bread at work.

It was also suggested that I should go to Switzerland to train to ice the elaborate cakes, but I decided not to go, because I would miss my mates and my football.

From being 15 years old I played Combination football, until injury forced me to quit at the age of 33. Later, when my son Robert became interested in football, we started going to watch the famous Accrington Stanley, at home and away. We are both still fans twenty odd years later.

When I was seventeen, I went back to Ramsbottom on my motor bike, to Aunty Alice's where I understood my brother Jimmy was living. As I knocked on the front door, Jimmy went out of the back door, and rode off into the sunset.

In 1967 I met Barbara and soon after we became engaged. Ten months after our engagement we got married on the 13th September 1969.

Thirteen was our lucky number.

I was still baking and Barbara was a clerk/ typist in a solicitors office, and we bought our house in Beech Street Accrington, where we still live today

On our third Wedding Anniversary(13th September) we brought home our first child-Judith Helen,and on the 13th of January, four and a half years later, Judith was joined by our son Robert John.

Our family was complete.

When I was a young child some one had asked me" what do you want to be when you grow up" and I had answered "a daddy".

MY AMBITION HAD BEEN REALISED.

Barbara and I have worked hard and have enjoyed a fairly good life, owning our own home, taking many holidays, in Gt. Britain and abroad, having cars and of course being blessed with our two lovely children, who have provided us with four lovely grand children.

During 1977, Social Services wrote to me and asked if I would like to be put in touch with my younger brother Stephen--- I agreed.

On the 27th June 1977, the day our son Robert was baptised, Stephen turned up at our house, but I had gone

Living in Hope

out. We did eventually meet up, and got on really well. He filled in some of the large gaps in my family history.

It was soon after that, that we met our sister Alice, and then we went over to Bury to meet Janey and Pauline,(two sisters who had been born to mum and dad after they had been re-leased from prison).

I was to meet my birth mother and father (Margaret Russell and George Hardman), I was very excited at meeting them for the first time. When I did, it was hard to see them as my mum and dad, as they were just an elderly couple, but they seemed alright.

I was glad that I had met them. I didn't feel much for them, but I did not have any animosity towards them at all. It just filled in a few gaps.

We only met Maggie and George a few times. Once was at Pauline's wedding in 1980, then 6 months later in 1981 our mother died. Stephen and I attended her funeral. George died of cancer 4 years later in 1985. Janie helped to nurse both of them (her mother and father) during their illnesses, it must have been very hard for her.

There was still something missing.

I knew that I had another two brothers and a sister somewhere, but I had no idea where to start the search.

When I met Pauline and Janey, they both had young families, so we went over to see them and their children every few months and phoned them occasionally. Pauline had two daughters and five sons, Janey had three sons.

Pauline attended Judiths wedding and wore a very striking red hat, she had to leave early because she was quite ill.

Her own wedding to Dave Shaw was brought forward to June due to her illness.

Barbara and I were buying her a two tier wedding cake, as her wedding present, and one week after Judith's wedding, we went to Pauline's house to take the cake so that she could put the finishing touches to the decoration. It was only three weeks to go to her own wedding, but we found that she was desperately ill, and had only a short time to live.

Dave and I went to a pharmacy to get her some diamorphine, as prescribed by the doctor in attendance.

After staying some hours, Barbara and I went home, but two or three hours later, Dave phoned to say that Pauline had just died.

I went over the next day and promised Dave, that I would help in any way. Barbara and Judith both offered to have all or any of the children for a few days, or for the odd week- end,to give him a break. He said that he wanted to keep the family to-gather.

About one year after Pauline died, his family was split up, due to Dave's neglect.

History seemed to be repeating it self.

Barbara and I spent two or three years trying to trace the youngest children, Lindsey was 11, Michael 10, Dave 6, Dell 5.We are now in contact with Lyndsay, who has a baby of her own, Michael is in the army, and Dave and

Living in Hope

Dell are with foster parents about 10 miles away from us

When the children were taken away from Dave, no one told social services that Pauline had other family, so we had no chance to offer our help

In 2001, I got a phone call from my sister Margaret, who had found my number. We arranged to meet at my grandson's birthday barbecue, but I was eager to meet her, and drove down to Liverpool to see her the following day.

Margaret had found Hughie, our eldest brother, so now there was only James to find. Margaret, Tom, Barbara and I went to the Rose and Crown in Ramsbottom to arrange a re-union for the 3rd of November, all we had to do was find James.

During a visit to Mount Street in Ramsbottom, we met a neighbour who remembered James, but she had no idea where he was now. Later that day, I got a phone call to say that she had just remembered that James was called Hardman and not Russell, as we had thought

Our daughter Judith went back on the internet and found a J. R. Hardman, who was living in Todmorden, Yorkshire. Judith and I went over to Todmorden to see him. As he opened the door, it was so obvious that he was my brother, we found out that it was his birthday, that very day.

What better present could we have given him, his whole family returned to him

When we met Hughie at his home in 2001 he was quite ill. Margaret came over from Liverpool to help as much as possible. Hughie deteriorated and was hospitalized.

The Re-union at the Rose and Crown was a wonderful day. We met the families of our brothers and sisters, took many photographs, enjoyed a lovely buffet and gained some very happy memories. Unfortunately Hughie was too ill to attend, Janey was also unwell, and of course Pauline had died. We all vowed to keep in touch, and do so.

Hughie had severe diabetes and suffered a stroke.

We all visited him as much as possible. Barbara and I visited as often as we could, but only for short periods of time, partly because conversation was difficult as I did not know him, I was only two when I last saw him. I also had just become ill with diabetes mellitus, which apparently runs in our family. Mum died from it, Hugh, Alice and Pauline also had the disease.

Eventually Hugh was moved to the Cliff, which is in a lovely setting, but he was unable to see very far, so could not appreciate the view or the impressive house.

When he went into hospital for the final time we continued our regular but short visits.

The morning after he died, Barbara and myself went to see him in the hospital chapel, and we saw what he would have looked like as a younger fit man.

He really did look serene we had only known him ill and in pain.

Living in Hope

The day after Hugh died, my foster brother Alan died, and their cremations were held at Accrington Crematorium, one after the other.

As I could not be in two places at once, Barbara, Judith and I went to the service for Hughie at the Crematorium and stayed on for Alan's service (we had lived as brothers for 50 years) so I did the best I could

Later that week, we went to Nottingham for the funeral of Sister Alice's son Shaun, whom we had known from a young boy. It was a very sad week for all of us.

Although some of the family have now died, my daughter Judith has emigrated to Australia, and Margaret's daughter Sue has gone to live in Spain. I am very happy to have met all my family, and it is wonderful to see the many similarities between us even though we have not been brought up together.

I am proud of the way our families have coped throughout our very different lives.

Part 7
Stephen's Story

CHAPTER 1

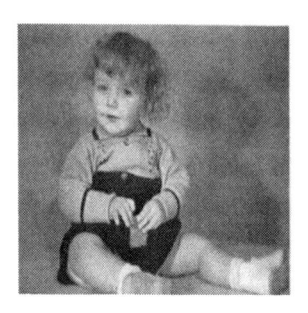

Stephen aged 18 months

My story takes you back in time to the winter's morning of 9th October 1948 Dawn was about to break over Fairfield Hospital in Bury. This was the day upon which I had decided to make my appearance.------STEPHEN RUSSELL--- had arrived, and entered this world. It was not to be a world offering security- it was into a world which was so different to the normal world (which most families take for granted.)

My destiny was to be trespassed upon, and my name and identity stolen. I, (Stephen), was the youngest of the Russell children. The others were Hughie, Margaret, Alice, Jimmy, and John, making a total of six.

More so, I was to be the last of the first family born to my mother (the late Margaret Russell).Another ill fated family was to follow as you will discover in due course.

My world started normally enough. My mother was admitted to Fairfield Hospital, Bury. It was a hospital that was to play a part to giving life to our family, and later taking some of the family away from us.

I had arrived into this world in an East Lancashire mill town, high on the moors, over the smoke drenched streets, with Bury and Ramsbottom nestling below. You will already have read of my arrival and transfer to Closes Farm, in my brothers and sisters reflections and recollections of 1948, and that I had returned to the farm in the loving care of my late mother(Margaret) and my brothers and sisters.

The old farmhouse had very few comforts, and would be very vulnerable in winter, but it was to be our future home, and a roof over our heads, to meet our personal needs at that time.

There would inevitably be hard times, but this was the aftermath of World War 2, after which food and clothing was still rationed even in the cities and mill towns, the length and breadth of the country, affecting almost every one in some aspect. A time when money was short because work was hard to find. The Russell family were no exception.

We never mistook the situation that winters at Buckhurst could become harsh and relentless, but it was to be our chosen new life, and we would have been prepared to manage the best we could. Our parents would have been looking long term.

Rome was not built in a day.

Living in Hope

They would have had visions of hens, geese and ducks producing fresh eggs, and livestock goats and cows for milk, with the land itself, producing hay for the livestock and vegetables for home use, and perhaps to sell on the local markets.

The summers, in the main, would have to be spent repairing the ravages of winter. The house and dry stone walling, would have been very vulnerable to frost damage at the high altitude.

Ready available brushwood would have provided fuel for heating and cooking. The family thought they had security but it was not to last.

Soon after my arrival in October 1948, the authorities started voicing the opinions that a significant move towards the serious consideration of removing the children from the farm, was to be a step in the right direction in their view, founded on what ever their beliefs.

You will have read how our family's world. was turned upside down, and how we were forcibly separated into oblivion as a family.

The seeds to the future chip on my shoulder had been sown. It has continued to grow every day for 58 years, and has grown to proportions that could supply every one of Harry Ramsden's famous chip shops.

Who peeled the potato to create this chip in 1948?.---Various misguided East Lancashire authorities.

Their misguided opinions instigated the court proceedings that persecuted my late mother and father, which resulted in custodial sentences being imposed and the ensuing care orders being obtained. Whilst my brothers and sisters were being ostracised to every point of the proverbial compass i.e. Ramsbottom, Liverpool, Accrington, and Nottingham under varying care options, I was destined for a new future over one hundred miles away from my brothers and sisters. I was despatched to a family in the ship building town of Barrow-in- Furness. It was to be a substitute roll to replace a still born baby girl for which they grieved the loss.

After 18 months they took my name Russell from me, and I was renamed with the surname Smith. I kept my Christian name of Stephen, which was now to be my only link with my past. They had not been happy at just fostering, they wanted to adopt me to make the situation more permanent. They applied to the Magistrates courts in Barrow but it wasn't to be straight forward and took 18 months.

My natural mother fought to have me returned to East Lancashire. After lengthy persuasion she finally gave up her fight for custody. From what I am told she fought long and hard, but I was adopted into the Smith family, and a new shorter birth certificate, with no previous family details, was issued in my name of Smith.

The committees, in their infinite wisdom, decided to enter my previous environment to split up my family. They created an ulcer so great, that after all these years, it still remains, and has only recently started to show signs of scar tissue for me, since our recent family re-union.

Living in Hope

It will unfortunately remain on our family's emotions permanently.

Because we were poor, the family would have been deprived of the chance to even consider seeking legal advice and representation. Our parents would have succumbed to the pressure mounted on them by the authorities. They would not have had the education to prepare their own defence against a Victorian regime full of religious convictions and beliefs.

I am sure all of the family will have suffered emotional mood swings and depressions of varying degrees at one time or another.

Some of my reflections on the chain of events that happened at Closes farm in 1948 have been as dark and grey as the unforgiving Lancashire moors on a cold, damp wet and windswept winters day.

Fate now dictates the speed at which the resurrected Russell family must now move forwards and onwards in our search for a united destination.

Each new day in the lives of the "Reborn Russell Dynasty" is equivalent of one full week in a conventional family. There will always be supplementary information of our past to uncover—considerable commuting into and out of East Lancashire, from our stolen identities, until all has been revealed, and any previously unknown or secret information on our family is allowed to be seen by all.

Only then can we re- establish the Russell surname once and for all. Yes, we are different and more unique than most families.

We will be recognised, and re-established because the Russell family have re-turned much stronger as one.

We can't physically turn the clock back (we all wish we could) but it is beyond the bounds of all possibility. What is not though, is the Russell dynasty re-establishing their family roots, and re-thieving their credibility.

We have resurfaced, re-grouped and returned with pride.

Before the youngest of the stolen children from Closes farm starts his personal story, may I add how privileged I feel to at least have met all of my family.

Some of the family were deprived of this opportunity, and only have sadness that in this life it was not a possibility for them.

With my late parents, the late Hughie and the late Pauline remembered I will begin my life story

CHAPTER 2
18 MONTHS TO 5 YEARS OF AGE

I was to be brought up as an only child. For what ever reasons my adopted parents never considered adding to their family with further adoptions. They were offered further adoption chances to add to the family but these they refused.

Dad made sure that I was aware that I was not their natural child. This he did at a very early age.

I remember that we had collected granddad's dog to take for a walk and he just came out with:-

You know how we went to the pet shop to choose Chummy, well we did the same with you. We had to choose, and we chose you. You can always be taken back. We could have had others as well, but one is enough.

I have never forgotten that conversation—cold and clinical.

We lived in a two up two down terraced property at 84 Island road, over looking the railway station that received two trains per day bringing ship yard workers to work from out lying areas. We had no bathroom extension, at that time they were not heard of. We did not even have a tin bath. I can recollect Mam standing me in front of an open fire place which appeared huge, the mantle piece being of solid wood and the surrounding area of pictured tiles. There she would wash and dry me until I reached school age. Dad worked in the ship yard as a timed served ships joiner but Mam never ever worked.

She took the roll of a Victorian house wife, which was to look after the home, while dad earned the wage packet.

I never started my school days at nursery, like some of the other children. I went straight into the Barrow Island junior school which was also on Island road at 5 years of age.

I left Barrow Island Junior School in the summer of 1960, having failed to qualify for either of the town's two prestigious schools. They were the grammar and technical schools respectively.

It was then a case of considering commuting to and from school. The Alfred Barrow county secondary school for boys was chosen because it was within walking distance of home. Mam and dad never owned a car, in those days cars were a luxury, not a necessity and neither could drive.

My first day at secondary modern was on the 13th of September 1960.A day that I had dreaded through out the summer recess. Older pupils, already attending the school had circulated rumours among the new starters (known as fags) about how they would be initiated on their first morning's attendance, when we were to have our heads shoved into the toilets, and then flushed, or were to be dropped into the basement. All our worries

Living in Hope

were to be unfounded. All went well, and I started in form 1 B, one of a class of 39.

At Christmas 1960, my father received my first school report, which he had to read, sign and return. My final term position was 11th, and exam position 14th, The form master wrote in his general remarks " tends to chatter, but has worked well, none the less. Stephen is keen, and helpful, and applies himself well". His punctuality is excellent, being absent once in a 120 days.

Whilst at school, my best subjects were science 3rd, English and art both 5th, and geography, my final position being 13th. The subject that I really excelled in, was rolling up blotting paper into a ball, dipping it into the ink well, and catapulting it onto the class room ceiling, where it stuck. An air vent in the ceiling was the target. We did this with a twelve inch ruler.

By the summer of 1961 I had progressed to 3rd in the class, to which the form master remarked ,"Stephen has now put work before chatter and his results have shown him to be a capable worker, I would like him to take more interest in sport".

I absolutely hated participating in sport at this time in my life. I had no interest whatsoever in any of the school's teams, whether it be rugby, football or cricket, and loathed even more cross country running events.

It was not to be very long before I qualified in one of my best subjects "forgery!" I started reproducing my parent's hand writing and signatures to the effect of:- "please excuse our Stephen from sport today because he has…..various reasons.." on a very regular basis, i.e. every time a sporting event occurred. I should have been nominated for a GCE with distinction and credits in this venture

My form master endorsed my hatred of sport when commenting in his summer 1962 report quoting "but his attitude to games leaves much to be desired.

Although playing football at school was loathed, I did like to go with father and grand father to watch Barrow AFC, who at that time were playing league football. The first game they took me to watch, was Accrington Stanley (away).!!!!!!

It got me into trouble at school, one term for following Barrow AFC. The club were having a really successful FA Cup run. They had earned a replay at home, in one of the later rounds. FA Cup fever swept the town, and father who had been off work, ill, and was recuperating, managed to acquire two adults, and one child ticket, for the match.

The game had to be played in the afternoon because the club did not have floodlights at that time.

Father told me to take the after noon off school, but what ever happened at school next day tell the truth. Returning to school the next morning I discovered that the head master intended to visit every class in turn, regarding the high absenteeism the previous afternoon. He came into my class room, and called for all the boys who were missing from school the previous afternoon to come and stand at the front of the class, forming a line.

Living in Hope

He then proceeded to asked each boy in turn where they had been and the list read, dentist sir, hospital sir, doctors sir and so on, until it came to my good self who had been told to tell the truth. Where were you at Smith to which I proudly replied, "the foot ball match sir" adding what a great game it was as well. A deadly hush descended in the class, all eyes monitoring the cane, which was suspended over the black board. I must have been the only one in the whole school to stand up and tell the truth. The head master ordered I be detained after school each night for a week to write hundreds of lines to the effect that I must not miss school work for football matches.

That was one lesson learnt it doesn't always pay to tell the truth.

It didn't end there, as dad was summoned to the school by the head master to explain his involvement in the incident.

Unlike most of the boys I never had any inclinations to follow any of the prominent clubs of the day like Man United Aston villa and Burnley. I did save pocket money and sent off to the bigger clubs for programmes , some of which I retain to this day. At the end of the day there was only one team-- Barrow AFC. When we went to the home games we always used to sit in the stand.

Returning to my summer report of 1962 I finished in 2nd position and qualified for a form prize which was a book token. I received a book of my choice on speech night when all the form prizes were awarded. The following term, I progressed from the B form to the A form joining all the teachers "blue eyed pets and swots" to whom I instantly took a dislike. My attitude reflected in future results.

My new form master made various remarks such as, "rather poor, there are many weaknesses, very disappointing, to very poor on the whole." This was February 1964, and I decided it was time to leave school and move on into the men's world, at the shipyard, to seek a trade. And so as I will mention later on in TRAINING REFLECTIONS, I put my foot on the first step of the ladder towards acquiring a trade.

Whilst at school I always spent my lunch breaks cycling to the town's railway station to catch a glimpse of the (one o'clocker) to London. This was well known to the local train spotters because it always had a prestigious engine to haul it south. Names like The Royal Scott, Britannia, Evening Star, to name a few. This interest was never to leave me as even today I travel regularly to my homelands of Bury ,Ramsbottom and Rawtenstall—home of the East Lancs Railway, which is a preservation society maintaining and running regular steam hauled trains.

It was common for the older generation to look after their parents in their twilight years, and our family was no exception. Mam and dad took in my dad's father(my granddad,) when I was about 11 years old, and I lost my independence of a room on my own, I had to share with my granddad.

Living in Hope

My large double bed was removed and my dad bought two single beds. I never had any say in what materialized and I hated the arrangement. At that time I don't think any one realized that Granddad was going to live to the age of 90.

It put a lot of stress on mum, who's own health deteriorated shortly after Granddad passed away. They thought that she had arthritis, but when she went to the hospital for X rays and tests, as an outpatient, she was kept in, and died 3 weeks later from Multiple Myeloma- a type of Leukaemia.

It was rumoured that it could have been Nuclear Fallout from Windscale when they had the large fire in the 1950's, but because the incubation period was many years it could not be proved or disproved. If this was the case:- was I with her at that particular time.

At 7,45am on the day Mam died, the chief of the Shipbuilding Security Police came into the workshop where I was working. I had just started at 7,30am, and I was given the news and told to take as much time off as was required.

I always remember cycling with my best mate to the local football ground-Barrow AFC- to obtain some autographs.

We cycled home, but after 8pm in those days the shops were shut. I had some small change in my pocket and decided to invest in a packet of salted peanuts. These we obtained from a brand new vending machine on Main street corner. I put 2 old pence in the machine and started to turn the handle, but it came down the wrong way, I put my finger over the box to correct it, just as a bar came down trapping my finger.

The Fire Brigade were called, and despite the objections of the shop owner, they decided to burn off the corner of the brand new machine, using their brand new propane gas cutting machine. I was released and taken to hospital. It hit the headlines in the local evening paper including my photograph.

I remember playing cricket on the playing field behind where we now live. One lad went in to bat and was bowled out –first ball, but he would not hand over the bat and ran home with it.

I led the "posse" arriving at his home a little later. The lad appeared with the bat in an aggressive manner and I being the leader of the gang under took to remove the bat from him. I took one blow from the bat across my face and ended up in Barrow hospital and as I temporarily lost the sight in one eye was transferred to an eye hospital in Lancaster. My vision returned later in the week.

While I was in Lancaster Hospital I remember having a bath run for me by a very stocky nurse, when I was ready I went into the bathroom and the nurse came in behind me and closed the door

" Hell " that was it, I was out of that bathroom like a shot. I was not into voyeurism at the age of 14.

CHAPTER 3
TRAINING

I left the Alfred Barrow Secondary Modern School at Easter 1965. I was not supposed to finish until the summer of that year. It caused an awful lot of friction between my family and school with a lot of threats being exchanged.

I knew the local ship yard started a few hundred apprentices to various trades in the September, and it was an advantage, and you received preference, if you were already employed by the company.

The company had vacancies for the office boys during the Easter period. If you were lucky you would be taken on to the companies books and assigned to a particular office. It also helped if your parents worked in the company to pull strings which were required for a good reference.

I was given a start in the marine estimating office- "brewing up" and replenishing supplies of tea, sugar, milk and coffee from the local shops, adding to this list any sundry items required such as cigarettes, tobacco, and sweets etc. In those days when the workforce had clocked on, it was not possible for them to nip out to the shops, they would have lost wages and so my position became important. I used to head straight to the Co-Op and put everything on my mother's Dividend Number boosting the annual amount paid to her. The more you spent the more you got back in bonuses. I have never forgot her number to date 21187. The shop used to write down the number on a long narrow receipt which you kept to check, hence it being called your "check no " Other duties included taking internal mail and messages to the various departments in the ship yard. This experience proved invaluable later on, giving you hands on experience of the ship building environment.

Once you were on the companies books you could then apply for a trade. You obtained an application form, and listed three choices in order of preference. I listed fitter /turner, electrician and welder.I did not fancy the welding because of all the fumes.

You had to work hard for the office you were assigned to and then approached the office manager for a reference. Successful employees were then offered trades before the summer school leavers applied.

Hence leaving at Easter.

I was offered an apprenticeship as a fitter/ turner and started on the 6th September 1965 and this took until the 5th of September 1970 to complete.

My Dad had received a letter from the company on the 16th November 1966 to say that I had satisfactorily completed the probation period has an apprentice fitter/turner and would be obliged if Dad and I would call at the Apprentice Training School, Bridge Approach, at three p.m on Monday 21st November 1966 to sign the agreement of apprenticeship.

Living in Hope

At 9 am on Monday morning, 6th September 1965, myself along with all the other new starters congregated outside the apprentice training schools.

Half were recruited for the engineering company, and half for the shipbuilding company. Some of the lads were to start as fitters ,like myself, whilst others took alternative trades, such as electricians, welders, sheet metal workers and machinists

We were ushered into the buildings, I was recruited to the engineering company.

Once inside and into the workshop area we were introduced to the chief training instructor, Mr Stringer, who made a short speech. Then we were split into a number of groups, each having its own instructor. My group was G and our names were called off a register by our instructor, Mr Blyton. We were each issued with a note book, on which our name, clock and locker numbers were written. We then went upstairs where the chief instructor, Mr Stringer, and a company director, Mr Topham, met us. After a speech by Mr Topham, Mr Stringer proceeded to give us some notes on the schools rules, which we had to copy into our note books, some of which read:-

Washing up time:-

If used correctly is 10 minutes before finishing time and you must return to your placc of work after wards.

Bicycle sheds:-

"Before entering the school grounds, dismount. at the gateway.

Language:-

No obscene language must be spoken in the works.

Recreation room:-.

It must be kept clean at all times, and also, all working shoes must be removed before entering.

P.T. gear:-

You are requested to obtain a vest, shorts and plimsolls

Overalls:- All overalls are to be worn for your own safety and must be worn correctly and so on.

In the afternoon we started chipping the block (steel) by hand with a hammer and chisel. This exercise was designed to toughen up the hands. We did this for the rest of the afternoon, and all day Tuesday. Imagine a complete set of recruits, hammering away all day, simultaneously, in the days when health and safety wasn't revered, we had no ear defenders.

Wednesday a.m., we went upstairs into the classrooms, and the morning was spent watching three films entitled fair " Oriana (a liner built at Barrow for the P and O company, plying its business between the U, K and Australia)

It showed Oriana being built on the slipway, the fitting out Berth on Buccleuch dock, and also sea trials on the Firth of Clyde.

The film "New Power" introduced us to the SultzerDeisel engine programme, Films were taken of it being tested in the testing bay, and also of it being handed

Living in Hope

over to British Railways. There was also film footage of the engines at work, in Sweden and France.

Wednesday P M.

On Wednesday afternoon, Mr Blyton our instructor took us on a tour of the ship yard starting off at the pattern shop. Many important parts manufactured in steel were made here, first in wood, to check if all the dimensions met requirements and also the moulds for the foundries.

Out side was a large suction tank, where all the saw dust was drawn into and stored prior to removal. Inside the building, we were given the opportunity to inspect the moulds, which were being made ready for delivering to the foundry area, via the test house where we were lucky enough to see them testing a chain to destruction point. A chain was gripped at both ends in a pit and pulled tight. As the strain increased a clock on the machine registered the force applied until the chain broke.

In an adjoining room were two apprentices who had just completed their twelve months at the school, they were machining test pieces

We were lucky once again, at the foundries. We arrived just in time to see them pour some molten metal out of a furnace, down a trough, and into a large ladle. The ladle was then transported by an overhead crane onto a wagon, which was then transferred to another bay by a squad of workmen.

The work men then scraped of all the impurities, and it was then poured into a mould.

Next was the engine smithy and the blacksmiths (no relation). There we saw ingots being heated in the furness / forge. Further along the workshop we saw the drop/hammers in action, thumping red hot pieces of metal into shape.

The next port of call was to be the general machine shop. Here we saw horizontal borers, drilling and turning machines, in fact machines of every size and description.

After this we transferred to the Sultzer diesel test beds, where we could inspect engines while they were running. The noise was terrific, you could not hear yourself speak, and had to wear ear protectors.

We crossed over into the engine assembly shop, were the engines were being assembled prior to testing.

Next on the tour was the engine shop where we saw machinery being assembled for soap factories, and next door was the North shop, where guns which were fitted to the foredecks of the war ships, were being assembled and tested.

After this, we returned to the training school. The tour had been very constructive and we had all learnt many interesting things. Then for the rest of Wednesday afternoon we re-turned to chipping the block.

Thursday was a very disappointing day, because we never received any pay, the company worked a week in hand, which was paid out at the holidays to cover the second week of the summer break.

Living in Hope

Again it was to be the case of more chipping, and then we were summoned to attend a lecture on first aid and artificial respiration.

By the end of the week many of the lads were in need of it.

Friday was to be a repeat of Thursday, more chipping. To-wards the end of the day I had managed to chip , file, and scrape the test piece to the prescribed dimensions.

I thought the school was a good idea, giving insights into various aspects of engineering, and the staff were very informative.

Soon it was to be finishing time, and time to clock off.

The first week was completed and it was time to wash, and change the oily bandages that were lagging all the cuts and bruises caused by missing the chisel with the hammer, whilst chipping endlessly.

We put on clean bandages, for the weekend.

The first week of my apprentice ship was over.

It was worth while looking forward, and giving the hands time to recover, ready for another week ahead.

I left the training school as Top Apprentice of the Intake

CHAPTER 4
WORKING LIFE

When I left the training school, I transferred to the tool room which was always regarded as the elite. I went on to do machining work and fitting on the Seltzer diesel program. In 1971 I transferred from the engineering side to the ship building.

I started work in the engine rooms of H.M.S Sheffield.(An A type destroyer) which was lost in the Falklands conflict, and sailed as part of the ships crew to Cambletown in Scotland. We did the ships measured mile on the Clyde, to see how fast she could go, and then on to Portsmouth.

When this contract was finished, I transferred to HMS Manchester another destroyer of the same class. I then went onto something very much larger- H.M.S Invincible , the country's first through deck cruiser. I believe it was described as a cruiser because government funding would not pay for any new Aircraft Carriers to be built.

I worked on the Invincible for a number of years, until she was completed and handed over at Portsmouth Naval Dock. I sailed with the ships crew to Scott Lithgow ship yard in Glasgow, where she entered the dry dock. We then sailed down to Wales for Missile and Gun trials

Living in Hope

and on to Portsmouth, where in the English Channel, Helicopter and Sea Harriers completed their trials.

I spent a lot of time commuting from the Hotel International to the Portsmouth dock yard each day.

I represented the ship building company as a guarantee engineer. What ever the navy wanted changing we did, and drew up the work on plans and sent them to the drawing office, for updating and costing.

From Invincible I progressed into Trade Related Paperwork on the Submarine Project working in the Reactor Dept., These records had to be very detailed and precise and put me in good stead for my next job which I applied for.

I transferred to the Trident Submarine Project as Production Control Engineer. I was responsible for ordering, from our U.K store, Submarine parts that were shipped from the U.S.A and supplying them to the various trades for manufacturing.

I joined an out of hours club –Vickers Armstrong motor club—and drove for them in rallies, with some success, winning quite a few trophies. I hand built and tuned my own engines, trying to surpass every thing that the whole Ford design team had achieved.

I put in for voluntary redundancy in 1991 because I was suffering a lot of pain to various joints from arthritis. This was granted and I now have my pension and freedom

On a lighter note, whilst working on HMS Invincible, we learnt that we would be a part of the ships crew, sailing with her from the Port of Barrow to Portsmouth Naval Dockyard. This meant that we would be accommodated in an hotel while finishing touches were made to the ship, prior to commissioning. All the talk amongst the lads on the shop floor was centred around the Portsmouth night life—pubs on every corner, and the famous Wednesday night "grab a granny night" at the Mecca dance hall.

So I, looking ahead and unable to dance a step, decided to enrol at my local Dancing School, so that I would at least know a bit.

Some how word reached the shop floor and the lads reacted.

One afternoon, I filled my tool bag with what I needed and set off to board Invincible, which at that time was on the slipway prior to launching. It was a good 5 minutes walk, and then necessitated climbing stairways, various passages and decks, down to the engine room.

Meanwhile (unknown to me) the lads had been down to the Joiner's shop and had two stencils made in the shape of a left foot and a right foot

I completed my work in the engine room, and set off back to the workshop. As I reached the side of the ship, I was greeted with large white footprints from the ship to my toolbox in the workshop. The full length of the dockside was painted in large left and right footprints numbered 1—2—3, 1—2—3, which I learnt to be the waltz steps, there were "hundreds of them".

Fortunately the management saw the humorous side of it.

Living in Hope

Another humorous note was when I learned that the company was to install its very first closed circuit TV camera with in the works. The company planned to install it on top of the large ship yard crane. Which dominated the sky line.

It concerned me more that from its position, it could look down into my garden, and I was not too pleased.

I approached the company with my concerns, and I will always remember saying to the manager "I don't want to pass through the gate house, were the monitor was to be installed, to be told that I was planting my potatoes up side down".

I partitioned other local residents ,involved the union regarding the invasion of privacy, and the local evening newspaper. I stood on the toes of the managers, and it caused a few rumblings at work.

The same squad of lads who instigated the "dock side dance" reacted once again, unknown to me.

They went down to the central stores and obtained some card board boxes, to make card board cameras, with card board tubing for lenses, and red plastic caps for the glass. These were assembled by my colleagues who took them to the paint shop, had them painted mat black with CCTV 1,2,3, painted on them. When I came off the ship all these cameras were arranged up on the roof girders, looking down on to my work bench and tool box.

When I entered the work shop, where every one was waiting, a loud cheer rang out.

It wasn't a place to be an introvert ,you had to take it in the good humoured sense it was meant, and I did "B------s".

This was on or about the Thursday ,by Saturday morning the national news papers had a "Big brother is watching you" article included

One night, while working away on Invincible in Portsmouth dock yard, we had returned to the comfort of the Hotel International. The lads had spruced up and congregated in the bar. We had teamed up with a squad of Canadian Helicopter pilots who were also staying in our Hotel. It was a case of who could stand their round of beer the best. The two teams were known as "the lads from up North" and the "whirly bird technicians from across the pond". It was decided that we would start on all the multicoloured bottles on the shelf behind the bar, working from left to right, having a tipple from each.

Half way through the proceedings it was decided that we would have some music. Abdul, the Arab owner had an electric organ in the snug, and we decided to switch it on. Unfortunately when we plugged it in, we could not get a sound out of it. An agitated Abdul came from the concert room ranting and raving. Someone had crossed the tropical fish tank containing Abduls prize tropical fish, with the organ's amplifier, and blew up the fish tank. Needless to say, fish was off most of our menus for the rest of our stay, opting for meat dishes only.

When Invincible returned to Barrow, I was on the food lifts –the mechanism that transfers the food from the fridges to the dockside. There were a few lads in the crew, and as the food went down onto the dockside, it was "one for us" and "one for the hotel" which had bought the food. I had to order a taxi to take me the few hundred yards home.

CHAPTER 5
COURTING AND MARRIAGE

As I have previously stated, I first noticed Sheila and her friends watching us playing football, in the school playground. As teenagers, we played every Sunday afternoon. One of the footballers had to baby-sit for one of his relatives, as they went out dancing most Saturday evenings. This gave the boys a chance to ask the girls around. Sheila, being one of the group, I asked her personally.

As the Saturday night progressed I made advances to Sheila's best friend Elaine. Even to this day, Sheila never lets me forget the events, and how could I. Elaine told Sheila on their way home. It was the very first time, or was it the second, or third, that I had felt the warmth of a girls flesh, some where between the neck and the waist:

After that I had the nerve to ask Sheila out for a date, a good start.

At 16 I started my apprenticeship as a fitter –turner and Sheila started as a time served engraver. She soon became the best in her department, and was then given the responsibility of engraving the ships' bells and presents for the regular flow of dignitaries, who came to the shipyard, to oversee various launches and functions.

Living in Hope

The list included the Queen, Prince Philip, Diana, Princess Margaret, and other Royals. There were also political figures like Margaret Thatcher, the list being endless.

Each one of them will have a personal memento of the function they attended, engraved by Sheila.

We courted until we got married at St. John's church in 1972.

In those days holidays abroad were in there infancy and often unheard of. We used to go off on coach trips to "exotic places" such as Edinburgh, Whitley Bay, and Chester Zoo.

At that time I had just bought my first boat, and shortly afterwards a brand new 175 cc BSA Bantam motorbike.

Before I was allowed to take the boat out on my own ,dad organized it for me to crew for a chap he knew, who had a lot of experience, and would never take safety for granted, while at sea.

I made a mistake one day that still haunts me. We had been to sea, and returned to the boats deep water mooring and secured the boat where we had left the boarding dinghy to row ashore. We made sure every thing was secure.

As the owner was locking the cabin I made what could have been three fatal mistakes.Firstly I put on my waders in preparation for landing on the beech. Secondly I untied the dingy before I boarded, holding on to the rope securing it as I got in. I should only have untied it after I was safely aboard and sat safely with the oars in position. The dinghy tilted with the sea coming right up to the top of the side of the dinghy. I lost an oar and drifted down stream. If I had gone completely in the water I would not have survived, wearing wading boots, as they would have filled with water and pulled me under and I never had my life jacket on either.

Three safety lessons learnt.

During this period my main hobbies were sea fishing, boating, and rally driving. I was a member of the Furness Fishing Association- sea section and also a member of the Barrow Island boating club. I had various boats, and invested in a Beach Side Shed, within the confines of the club.

My first boat was on a mooring in mid channel, to which I had to row out by dinghy, but later I used an off-shore speed craft, which I used to tow to the sea on a trailer and then launch it. The dinghy gave me very many sleepless nights. I used to lie awake in bed on stormy ,wet and windy winters nights hoping all was well. Unfortunately on one of these nights, the boat broke it's moorings and drifted down the sea channel between Barrow and Halley Island and was only saved by an old sea salt.

Noticing what had happened, he risked his life by rowing out and towing it back. One of the seats was washed up on Road Island(ten miles away down stream)

Living in Hope

This convinced me to take the second option and buy a trailer- mounted out fit, which was a lot less worry as it was brought home after each trip, and locked safely in the garage.

This boat and I were not without our moments.

I was about 7 miles off shore on a sunny afternoon, the lines were baited and over the side, when a sea mist suddenly descended. It was just like some one turning down the dimmer switch on the living room light. My Royal Navy jersey became white and wet with water vapour. Quite a lot of boatmen were caught out that afternoon, and it became worse when darkness descended

The mist prevented me from seeing the lighthouse on the southern tip Walney Island, and panic arose. After a while I noticed what I thought was the lighthouse and I estimated it to be approximately 2miles to the south.

That was the signal for the fastest outboard motor start in the world. I pulled up the anchor and headed for the lighthouse. It turned out to be a cabin light on another boat and I nearly cut it in half, as it was only 100 yards away. This boat had a radio and radar and was slowly sailing home.

It gave the owner and I quite a start, but as I did not know my way through the sea way in the mist, he offered me a safe journey in his boat, towing mine behind.

I was that glad to be aboard a bigger boat, that when I jumped aboard, I had left the engine running.

It had not gone unnoticed by the crew who had taken me in, and I was never allowed to forget it.

Sheila and I used to spend most evenings and some weekends (weather permitting) sailing down to Piel Island which was almost at the southern end of Walney Island towards Morecambe Bay, and once there we would fish and cockle.

We purchased our first house,(22 James Watt Terrace) twelve months prior to our wedding, and fully modernised it. It was a very spacious, three bed roomed Victorian terrace house and cost us £2300. It was nice to have a place to call our own.

Our wedding took place at St Johns Church on Island road, the same road I had been brought up on, at No 84.

After settling in for a few years, Sheila became restless at living in a built up area, and yearned for a bit more space and a garden, like her parents home at Cricketfield Cottage where she had been brought up with her pet nanny goat—Lulu.

I was only too glad to be leaving Island Road, I needed to move on. Perhaps with hindsight a little too quick and enthusiastic.

We scoured the property market in the surrounding countryside, but as we were both working full time at the shipyard, we had to consider commuting to and from work

Sheila's parents home had become too much for them to maintain, and as they did not really want to move

Living in Hope

away, we decided to buy the house and a 30 ft caravan as an extension to the living accommodation. The caravan was positioned adjacent to the house for Sheila's parents to occupy and we moved into the house, (selling James Watt Terrace). This remained the same for many years--- Sheila's father (Walter) died here and her mother (Norah) decided to move into a flat.

After our marriage in 1972, we strove to fulfil the ambitions that most people had,--- holidays abroad. We sold the motor bike, and bought our first car, a Lord Nuffield Special, (Morris Minor to the uninitiated). We kept the boat and enjoyed the beach life. Sheila shared this interest, as her father and uncle both had boats in the same club, at one time or another.

Her father spent a lot of time in the Merchant Navy, working on tugboats and dredgers, and later became a deep sea diver, on the docks.

As the marriage developed, we both found out just how much we were two opposites, and ended in divorce in 1983. we are still together though after 34 years, but for how long it is difficult to say.

CHAPTER 6
CRICKET FIELD CAT SANCTUARY

In the 1970s we established the above sanctuary at our home at Cricket field cottage and we are still running it to-day.

Ever since Shiela and I returned to Cricket field cottage from James What Terrace in the 70s we have dedicated a lot of our time financing, assisting and homing stray and abandoned industrial cats.

Most have made their own way to us from the adjacent ship yard, which has been in steady decline. Many of the work force were made redundant, and out fitting sheds were demolished to save on over heads.

The ship yard population depended on the work force to feed them, and they relied on the sheds for shelter.

When I took voluntary redundancy in 1991 it allowed me more time to help the feline population.

Our activities attracted the attention of our local evening news paper, and they decided to include an article on our efforts. Quoting from this article will explain what we have achieved.

Head line:-
"Peaceful haven in perr-fect setting"
and it read:-

Living in Hope

"Through the key hole"

"Before the industrial era, Barrow island was a peaceful haven of tree lined avenues , and a perfect cricket pitch. Phil Smith (no relation) finds a corner which harps back to those times.

The end of Buccleuch Dock road is hardly the place you would expect to find a haven, but after half a mile of pot holed road, lined on both sides with industry, you come across Cricket Field Cottage.

The cottage is painted white, and is a 117 year old oasis, set in a garden of magnolia, cherry, chestnut, beach and willow trees, together with currant bushes, blue bells and daffodils, and lit by a copper Victorian street lamp.

Cricket field cottage is the home of Steve and Shiela Smith, who have lived there since the early 1970s, and the cats since three years ago, when Steve was made redundant from his job as a fitter at V.S.E.L, after thirty years. He noticed that others were out of a job too. The wild "mousers" living in the sheds which Vickers were demolishing on the opposite side of the road, were redundant, but also homeless.

So he decided to dedicate his enforced retirement to looking after them.

He bought a £400 shed, fitted it with a cat flap, baskets and cushions, and spends £600 a year, filling it with food, and heating it from gas cylinders, as a refuge for the cats.

Steve and Sheila have about 20 or so regulars, who visit the shed and garden plus another seven who live with them in the cottage.

"Most of them are wild, and don't like being touched, but they come and go as they please," said Steve, "When they lived in the Vickers's sheds, the workers would feed them, but after the redundancies, there was nowhere for them to go. Some of them are about 20 years old, and even if someone was willing to look after them, they would never settle for being "house cats"

The presence of cats, does not seem to bother the birds, who also flock to Cricket Field Cottage

Doves, starlings, sparrows, and magpies all frequent the house (attracted by the trees), and some of them nest and breed under the eaves.

Steve and Shiela moved into the house, because it was handy for Steve's work. He simply had to walk across the road. Steve said that when he came here, the garden was just an over grown field, but he planted trees, and put in some green houses and now the place more or less looks after its self.

If birds, cats , and greenery are welcome, Steve is a little more wary of human interlopers.

Visitors are expected to stand at the front garden gate, and pull a string to ring the bell. Even the postman has been given a special box at the gate. to leave letters ,and a notice warns off sales men, and religious callers.

"We like to live quietly, wouldn't you?" said Steve, who's friendliness belies his words.

Living in Hope

The cottage was built in 1881 for managers of the Furness Railway Company, when the company owned Barrow Island.

History books say that before industry encroached, the Island was a delightful enclosure of tree lined walks, playing fields, and the most picturesque cricket ground in the North of England. Even the world famous W. G. Grace played there. Hence the name of the house.

Industry may have wiped out most of the beauty of Barrow Island, but Steve and Shiela are keeping their corner as a little bit of paradise."

The article also depicts two photographs, one of their house and garden, and the other of myself at the garden gate.

It featured in the Evening Mail of Saturday April 18th 1998 and I have included it in my story to give an insight into my life at the cottage

CHAPTER 7
THE SEARCH FOR MY FAMILY

I decided to start a search for my family in the early 1970's and during my initial enquiries for details of my adoption, I was advised and went to Kendal for counselling, mainly due to the length of time lapsing. I discovered my original name had been changed from Russell to Smith and I was born in Ramsbottom, Lancs., and my Mam was a pensioner and lived in Bury, Lancs.

I decided to travel around the local sub post offices in the Bury area, researching the name Russell. After many calls I finally found one in Tottington Road, where some one knew of my family's whereabouts in Hazel Ave

I visited the Hazel Avenue council estate, and after various enquiries found Mam's house.

Amazingly, I found that there was a second family of Russell---Janey and Pauline, who were also my sisters. They were born after Mam had been released from prison. Mam lived with Pauline in Hazel Ave, and Janie lived directly opposite.

It was from here that I learnt that John my brother was living in the Accrington area, I forwarded this

Living in Hope

information to the Salvation Army who were already trying to locate my sister Alice's where about.

I then received a telephone call from my brother John in Accrington, who informed me that the Salvation Army had contacted him, and would he like to make contact with his natural family.

He had been fostered into the Caple family in Augusta Street, and had no information on his family's where about. John was agreeable to my request, and we arranged to meet at his parents home, very shortly afterwards, John brought his family to Barrow-in _Furness to meet my family, and we kept in regular contact.

Shortly after, the Salvation Army made contact with our sister, who was found living in the Nottingham area. Alice rang me and we arranged a meeting in Nottingham. This was successful and Alice returned the visit, travelling to Barrow to meet my new family.

After this visit we all arranged to visit Pauline and Janie, also meeting our natural mother.

After 58 years the family had started to re group.

It gave me great pleasure when Pauline asked me to give her away at her forthcoming marriage. After the church wedding ,the family attended the reception and family news was exchanged.

The next time the family was to meet together again was tragically to be at our Mum's funeral.

Mum was diabetic, and had to have her leg amputated due to gangrene setting in, an illness from which she never recovered. When mum died, Alice, John and I attended mum's funeral The cortege assembled at Pauline's home where the vicar attended for a small service. As tradition dictated Mam's coffin was laid in the front room, for the family to pay their respects and farewells.

Mum was interred in the family grave in Ramsbottom cemetery with her late sister Alice (a grave into which our late brother Hughie's ashes were to be scattered).

In the interim period, I received a letter from our youngest sister Pauline, informing me that she intended to remarry, and we were invited to the wedding which was to take place at Bury Register Office within the Town Hall on the 27th June ----.My brother John, having the honour of being Best Man. Shortly after receiving the wedding invitation, we received the tragic news that Pauline had been diagnosed as having terminal cancer, to which she wasn't to survive, and died before her wedding could take place. I travelled to Bury for Pauline's funeral, and pay my last respects. Pauline was buried in her Wedding Dress, looking as radiant as she looked in life.

After the funeral service, the cortege proceeded to Ramsbottom Cemetery where Pauline was interred.

Unfortunately the trail went cold, and there was to be a huge gap in time before Margaret, Hughie, and James were contacted, but fate dictated that it had to happen sooner or later

CHAPTER 8
THE FINAL CHAPTER

Now going into the final chapter of my life.I reflect with the question "when you are given only one life, why did mine have to be an imperfect one?"

I now have my family around me , the family that I have been deprived of for almost the entire life.

It felt like I had been given a life sentence, and only now, I am on parole for the rest.

No one knows what will happen next, and I only hope that if and when the cards are re shuffled, and redealt in the next world, I am dealt a hand containing a few high cards with a couple of Jokers thrown in.

I've had a lot of bad cards in my hand in this life, which a lot of gamblers would have stacked a long time ago

As a family, we have all re-visited Closes Farm, as one unit, seeking comfort and reassurances.

Even to-day a large part of our family emotions and feelings are still at Buckhurst ,luring us back at frequent intervals to try and seek answers to unanswered questions.(Questions that remain haunting the family as to what happened in1948).The family were split up and the Russells would adopt several family mottos one of which would be "where ever we all are this is us, and we will return, and this we did."

We returned as one reborn family, Margaret from Liverpool, Alice from Nottingham, James from Todmorden,(Yorkshire),John from Accrington,(Lancs,) and myself Stephen from Barrow-in-Furness,(Cumbria).Regrettably Hugh had departed this life a few months after sustaining a short illness, but he joined us in spirit. This we made sure of, he was not to be omitted nor was Pauline's or our late parents memory.

At our family re-union every one asked questions of each others past, Hence the individuals personnel motivation of each family member in compiling this book, recording details of our lives, and how we each lived since were taken into care, up to the re-union in Ramsbottom.

Now we can all refer to the accessible chronicles to answer our questions and catch up on each others past.

Margaret, Alice, James, John, myself, Margaret on behalf of the late Hugh are all making their own contributions.

CHAPTER 9
PERSONAL REFLECTIONS

Moving on after writing the final chapter to my life story, we come to the post mortem. The reunited families have all bonded extremely well. We have become much closer and stronger. You will have read previously how I had always lived my life in the fast lane, enjoying endless material items such as cars, boats and holidays, but there was always an element of despair and loneliness at losing my identity.

Now having rediscovered my identity, it is time to move forward and look to the future. Now there is love, happiness and hope, with new birthdays, and anniversaries to celebrate. There will always be very special events, such as new arrivals to the family

None of us can forget the past it will always serve as a reminder but we must move on.

Let the happiness flow and long may it well prosper

Part 8
Why?

CHAPTER 1
MARGARET'S SEARCH FOR THE REASON WHY

March 17th 1949.

I start back to the day when I was taken out of school, at Buckhurst, by two ladies whom I did not know. They had said that they had seen my Mum, and that it was alright to go with them.

Much later, I was to find out that my entire family had been taken.

WHY AND FOR WHAT REASON?

I can not remember Mum ever being cruel, or hitting us. So again I ask WHY?.

When I managed to trace my family, I got talking to my brother Stephen, who had been adopted by a couple, who lived in Barrow-in- Furness Cumbria. Stephen said that his Dad had told him, that Mum had been sent to Prison, for neglect of her children, and said he had believed him, as he was a very religious man so took his word as true. This I could not take in, Mum was never cruel to us. I knew Mum had not had much money, but that doesn't count up as cruelty, we were happy.

I told my sister, Lilian, about what Stephen had said, and she told me that unless it had been registered in a court hearing, to take no notice.

I still could not rest, so one day James my brother, Tom my husband, and I, went up to the Manchester Records Office, and asked could we see the records book of court cases, for 1949. We went right through the book, and found nothing. I was so relieved.

The following week, I said to Tom, that some thing was niggling at the back of my mind, and could we go up and see Kevin Mulley at the Bury Archives. So off we went. What I was hoping to find, I do not know. But Kevin suggested we try the Library in Ramsbottom, as they had a copy of a newspaper, called the Ramsbottom Observer. We thanked Kevin, who has been a great help to us right through our search, and headed off to Ramsbottom, yet again.

When we arrived, we spoke to a lady called Sue, who has also been a tremendous help we told Sue what we were looking for, and she then brought the newspaper for the year 1949. She set it up for us, and left to get on with her work. We went through page, after page. Tom said I don't think there is any thing here, but I had to keep going a couple of more pages.

Suddenly in print, was the news I had been dreading to find.

I just sat and cried, as I have never cried before. Sue came over to see what the matter was. When she read it, she could not believe it. She just got hold of me, and she

Living in Hope

cried. She said she was so sorry, after all the searching, to find this.

My Mum had been punished, for not having the resources to provide for us.

I feel so sorry, for what happened to Mum. Losing her children was trauma enough, without going to prison. It must have broken her heart.

I found out, through my search, that Mum had met up with a man, who I believe sold all our Grandparents furniture, to pay for his drink problem. When our Auntie Alice died, our cousin Fred, gave Mum her furniture, but this man George, was seen out side the second hand shop, selling the furniture that Fred had given to Mum. Fred never bothered with her again. What Mum saw in this man I will never know.

I was also to find out that Hugh had traced Mum when he came out of the Army. and helped her as much as he could. He went to live with Mum, who was now living in Bury, to try and sort out the money problems. But it was always the same. It ended in this mans pocket, for the pub.

Hugh did not like this man, at all. Apparently, when mum came out of prison, she stayed with him and had two daughters to him, Janie and Pauline. I never met Pauline. She died before I had traced my family, I did not know I had another two sisters.

Hugh said he went to visit Mum one night, and George was attacking one of the girls on the stairs. Hugh said if he touched her again he would be sorry. He then picked George up and hung him on a door coat hook, and left him there.

I also now know that Stephen, John, and Alice had traced Mum some years before, and went to Pauline's wedding. They sat opposite Mum, but never asked Mum any Questions about her life. They said she never mentioned her family. All she ever told Janie was that she had another family, some where, but did not know where they were

During my search, relying completely on my memory, I managed to retrace my steps, back to Kirkham Children's Home. While there, I was given a chaps name, who had once stayed there. His name was Kevin Walsh. He had done a great deal of research about the home, and the children who were placed there. I asked Kevin if he had found my name on the list which he had put together. He told me my name was not on the register, nor that of my sister Alice, but he said to try Lancashire Records Office. This I did, and bingo, my name was there, -- not only mine, but that of my brothers John and James, and my sister Alice. The dates we were boarded out, were there, but James could never remember being in a home, but the proof was there, for him to see, including the name of the home he was sent to.

While in Kirkham, I found that the school I attended was Wesham School. I asked the Headmaster if he had a register dating back to 1949, and could he, if he had time, take a look to see if I attended the school. He asked his Secretary to have a look, and there was my name,

Living in Hope

and class number 11. Up to now, I had had no proof that I existed before the age of 11. We then went back to the home, and told them that I had attended Wesham School in 1949. I asked who was the Matron who had been in charge, when I was there. It was a Mrs Barfield. I wrote to Kevin Walsh, and told him what I had found out. He in return, sent me a list of all the children who had been in the home

My next search was for the people, who had taken us, on 17th March 1949. Tom and I asked Kevin Mulley, if he had any idea were the log book from Buckhurst would be. Kevin said it was at the Archives. Another trip up to Bury. We met Kevin, and he got the book out for us, and there it was, the names of the people involved. The names of the people and departments who had been responsible for breaking up my family

Out of all the people I tried the Social Services at Preston and as far as Lancashire no one had any information on, me up to now I still had no medical records up to the age of 11 years of age I have also tried the NSPCC as far as London, I am told that all records of children who are fostered when they reach the age of 21 the records are destroyed which I think is totally wrong without the persons consent I think we should be consulted. And shown the documents first and then decide what we want to do with them we should be able to make that choice.

Part 9

CHAPTER 1
THE REUNION

Written By Margaret

James Alice Margaret Stephen John

All the family, but one, had been found. We still had to find James.

We decided to have a re-union. John, his wife Barbara, and Tom and I went to Ramsbottom to the Rose and Crown Hotel, not far from where Auntie Alice had lived, to see if we could have the re-union there. We booked it for the 3rd of November 2001.

Tom and I had been told that James had moved to Baxenden and worked at Holland's pie factory. We went along and asked if they kept records of employees and explained what we were trying to do, they said to leave it with them and they would get back to us, what we did not realize was that James could have changed his name if he had been adopted. We had a phone call from them to say that they had no records of any one with the name of James Russell. But we did not give up looking.

All we had to do was find James, the brother who all those years ago I had said I would not be long. I was only 56 years late.

.We had been told that James may have moved to Yorkshire, so we looked at the telephone directory for that area, and came across a number that we tried a few times but kept getting the unobtainable tone.

One day my daughter Sue and I went shopping, when we got back my granddaughter Gemma was shouting for us to hurry up, as my brother John was on the phone, I said to Sue I think James has been found, we ran into the house John asked me to sit down and yes they had traced James ,Johns daughter Judith had been on the internet they had found an address in Todmorden,in Calderdale Yorkshire, so they decided to go and check before they told anyone what a shock when John and James stood face to face, after all these years the phone number we had all been trying had been James but he had changed it a couple of weeks earlier

When John rang to tell me, he also said it was James birthday, the 19th October, what a day.

Living in Hope

I decided to have a cake made for the re-union, and went to David's in Crosby, who made cakes for the Royal Family. I mentioned it was for a re-union and David's Mum asked what kind of re-union it would be. As I explained, she said , you will need a bigger cake, but the price will be the same, the rest of the cake will be on us. She then asked what my brothers and sisters name were, as she would inscribe their names on the cake. David's Mum asked if for a finishing touch would I like to put a verse on, I decided to put:-

There will be no sadness any more, no pain to bring us sorrow, instead we can look forward to a brighter world to-morrow.

The day arrived for the re-union. John was going to pick up Hugh.

we all arrived at the Rose and Crown. Alice, Bill, and Shaun, (Alice's son}, and our Stephen arrived at the same time.

Carrying the cake, I walked in, and there in front of me stood James, (I nearly dropped the cake, the manager of the Rose and Crown took it off me just in time)I thought I had shed all the tears I had, but when I saw James, we just held one another and cried..

The only one who could not make it was Hugh. He was not well enough to come.

Miss Choudrey had arranged for a photographer to come along, and write a story on the re-union, and take some photos, it was a lovely day to remember..

During the afternoon, we all walked up to see the house where Auntie Alice had lived. Graham, the chap who had bought the house, invited us all in to have a look. What memories it held for us. We also went to see the woodland, where we all played as children. I will never forget that part of my childhood, they were happy days..

Down the road from the Rose and Crown was a duck pond, I took all the young children down to see the ducks, we all had to walk in single file. I was like the mother duck with all her ducklings

Since I have found all my family, my name has been Mother Hen, because, apparently when they were all small, I was always there for them.

As the day came to a close every one said what a great day it had been and that we must all stay in touch we all formed a circle and sang you will never walk alone which John said was now the family song..

Alice Bill Shaun stayed over night in their campervanI felt so sad to leave every one I thought that I would never see them again so early next morning Tom and I went up to Ramsbottom to the Rose and Crown and surprised Alice and Bill we all spent the day together, we decided to try and find the cottage but Alice only had sandals and the lanes where to wet so we abandoned the idea, the time came for us to leave for home so Alice went back to Nottingham and Tom and I came back to Liverpool.

We all phone one another and see each other as often as possible,

Living in Hope

I believe that God has a plan for every one for when Hugh needed help tom James Sandra and I and his nieces Gaynor Sue ,Gemma and his little Aimee, where there for him The only other persons apart from Hugh that I missed so much at the re-union was Mum and Dad,

I hope Mum as you look down from above you are smiling because we had done the one thing that you were not able to do which was to re-unite our family again.

We will never know the truth about what caused Mum and Dad to separate but I know from the bottom of my heart that I still love them.

Mum died in 1981 aged 67, and Dad died in 1960 aged 53.

I never saw my mum and Dad again after 1949 when I was aged 10.

People say that time heals I still shed tears for all those lost years without my beloved family when for 56 years, I prayed when the time was right I would find them all again. God willing

WE ARE ONCE AGAIN A HAPPY FAMILY

ACKNOWLEDGMENTS

We would like to give a huge THANK YOU to the following, who without their help we would never have been able to become a family again.

Sue the Librarian of Ramsbottom Library.
Kevin Mulley archivist at Bury Archives (later at National Archives Kew)
Pete and Marlene Bonie from Bacup
Jenny of Rossendale Free Press
Miss Choudrey of the Bury Times
Friends of St Paul's Church Ramsbottom.
Ged Ashe - who after hearing our story invited us as a family to look around the cottage we once called home before being taken into care.
Anne of Kentergern house for finding all my Father and Brothers Army Records
Margaret, Alice, James, John, Stephen and the late Hugh owe you all a great big

THANK YOU

Printed in the United Kingdom
by Lightning Source UK Ltd.
134887UK00001B/10-33/P